NC 9/10

A *Royal* HOME *in* WALES

LLWYNYWERMOD

MYDDFAI
CARMARTHENSHIRE

By Mark Baker

MMVIII

Published by Accent Press Ltd – 2008

ISBN 9781906373603

Copyright © Mark Baker 2008

Printed and bound in the UK

Cover and internal design by Ian Findlay

The sepia pen and ink drawing shown on the front cover of this publication
was commissioned by the Georgian Group in 2008 for presentation to
HRH The Prince of Wales. It was executed by the North Wales based artist,
Ceri Leeder, who had worked previously with the Welsh Historic Gardens Trust
in producing reconstructions of Llwynywermod featured in this publication.
Courtesy of the Georgian Group.

Dedicated to the memory of Christine Heap

Contents

Fig. 1. *An antique settle with watercolours of Caernarfon Castle during the investiture of HRH The Prince of Wales. Courtesy of Wales News Pictures.*

Fig. 2. *A detail of the 'Llwynywormwood Park'*
watercolour dated 1870, showing the mansion
house during its prime. Courtesy of Thomas Lloyd.

Owners of Llwynywermod

EARLY SEVENTEENTH CENTURY TO PRESENT DAY

WILLIAM WILLIAMS

DAVID WILLIAMS

DANIEL WILLIAMS ?? – 1765

DAVID WILLIAMS 1765 – 1785

SIR GEORGE GRIFFIES-WILLIAMS 1785 – 1843

SIR ERASMUS GRIFFIES-WILLIAMS 1843 – 1870

CAROLINE BEAUMONT 1870 – 1907*

JULIANA GRAVES-SAWLE 1870 – 1884*

JULIA RASHLEIGH RODD 1884 – 1913*

MARIANNE GRAVES-SAWLE 1884 – 1913*

AMY TREVANION NOON 1884 – 1913*

THOMAS WILLIAM ROGERS 1913 – 1923

HETTY ISAAC (NÉE ROGERS) 1923 – 1960

DAVID THOMAS LEWIS 1960 – 1963

EDWARD AND GILBERT STROUD 1963 – 1998

JOHN AND PATRICIA HEGARTY 1998 – 2006

THE DUCHY OF CORNWALL 2006 ONWARDS

*BENEFICIARIES OF SIR ERASMUS GRIFFIES-WILLIAMS

LIST OF ABBREVIATIONS

CA – Cambria Archaeology
CRO – Carmarthen Record Office
H – Mr and Mrs Hegarty
HMSO – Her Majesty's Stationery Office
JB – Jean Baker
KC – Kenwyn Church

KHL – King's Head, Llandeilo (National Trust Office)
MB – Mark Baker
NC – Noon Collection
NLW – National Library of Wales
NT – National Trust
OS – Ordnance Survey
PRO – Public Record Office
RCAHMW – Royal Commission on the Ancient
     and Historical Monuments of Wales
TL – Thomas Lloyd

ACKNOWLEDGEMENTS

The author wishes to thank the following persons and bodies
for all the assistance he has received.

Carmarthen Record Office and Town Library
Ceri Leeder
Colin Noon and Family
Craig Hamilton
Denbighshire Record Office, Ruthin
Design2Print, Llandudno
Douglas Mann
The Duchy of Cornwall and Clarence House
Dr Manon Williams
George Hext
Itaca Community Youth Project, Abergele
Ian Findlay and family
Jean Baker
John and Patricia Hegarty
Melissa Beattie
Michael Tree
National Library of Wales
The National Trust
Philip May
Richard Broyd
Rosemary Rooney
Royal Commission on the Ancient and Historical
     Monuments of Wales
St. Kenwyns Church, Truro and Diocesan House, Truro
St. Michael's Church, Myddfai
Stacey McCarron
Stephen Batsford, Newton House
Welsh Historic Gardens Trust
Jeremy Rye
Judith McSweeny
Ann Carter
Hazel, Bob and everyone at Accent Press
The Georgian Group, in particular Robert Bargery
Thomas Lloyd
Mark Davies of Llandeilo
University of Wales, Bangor Library and Archives
Cardiff University Library and Archives

Foreword

by Thomas Lloyd OBE

Chair of The Historic Housing Association in Wales

*S*ome old houses leave their history in abundance, with centuries of deeds, documents and drawings carefully catalogued in the local record office and books or learned essays recounting the achievements of their family. In west Wales, where the late Francis Jones, Wales Herald and Carmarthenshire County Archivist for long held sway, such a house would have been the subject of one of his many detailed contributions to a history society journal and there would have been no need to inquire further.

Such collections are sadly in the minority. Changes of ownership, the break up of estates, fires or flooding cellars, thoughtless disposal – bonfires were common – when houses were finally abandoned in distress between world wars, even the more recent attraction of flogging them for cash (vellum deeds do make such lovely lampshades), have all deprived the historian of far more than actually survives.

Llwynywermod is one such ancient but archivally deprived place, tucked away in the secluded hills above Llandovery, reclusive now, though a place of pride and ambition two centuries ago. Indeed so forgotten has it been since the late nineteenth century that not a single photograph or postcard of it with its roof on has ever come to light: no one thought it was worth dragging a heavy camera up there, despite its serene setting, lake and panoramic views. It is not an encouraging start to a research project. Yet it is not as if the family did not make a noise. Their baronetcy in 1815 put them at the top of county society (grander peers being an almost non-existent species here), while the head of the family fifty years later was not far off adding a bishop's mitre to the family honours.

All that seemed to be known in recent years in west Wales was what several of them looked like, thanks to a descendant, long settled in south-west England (and now deceased) donating to the National Trust some of the family portraits that she owned,

Fig. 3. *The gothic stone mullion window of the new dining room at Llwynywermod. Courtesy of Wales News Pictures.*

three of which the Trust had hung in the regional office in Llandeilo. The mansion itself is shattered and hard mentally to reconstruct, with its several building phases and irregular ground plan; the lake has silted up; the front drive is closed. Only the enormous eighteenth-century barn, kept in use for farming purposes in the old home farm yard, bears any lasting testimony to the former capacity of the place. Who were these people? What were they about?

This fascinating and surprisingly ample volume is a tribute to the research skills and tenacity of Mark Baker, who has looked and indeed travelled far and wide to reconstruct this record from many different sources. Better still, he has traced a surviving branch of the owning family, who hold other portraits and heirlooms. Indeed, this book is an object lesson in how a history can be put back together even when the principal resource has gone. The interlocking network of relationships and social interaction carries one family into the records of many others, while public careers are charted in the newspapers, journals and official records of the day.

Being titled, the Llwynywermod family were invited to have their detailed genealogy set out in the endlessly updated volumes of Burke's Peerage and Baronetcy and, in the ludicrously snobbish atmosphere of Victorian Britain when ancestry counted for more socially than endeavour, there were other places to extol one's inherent worth and gilded curriculum vitae, such as in Nicholas's Annals of the Counties and County Families of Wales (1872). Privately published books of family record were also common, with widely constructed family trees, unfolding accordion-like from between the pages, pulling in every remote connection to even grander families: the volume about the related Thackeray family (as of the famous author) has turned out to be a rich source of material for this story for the late nineteenth century. The Welsh passion for genealogy in the much earlier period of the Tudors and Stuarts has also provided details for the front end of the story.

In the end it is a sad tale of decline and heart-breaking abandonment of the ancestral acres – the usual story in fact of the majority of the lesser county families in Britain in the first fifty years of the last century. The rise and fall of Llwynywermod is typical of thousands: successful careers and marriages raising them up in the eighteenth century, hedonistic living eroding the position in the careless early nineteenth and the debts piling up under self-deluding Victorian squires, who assumed that the ownership of land was always going to see them through, despite the crippling expense of their liveried households. They did not see it coming, just as (writing this in the middle of a terrifying financial crisis with banks bankrupting weekly) we still do not now.

Mark's achievement has been to put a forgotten estate back on the map. More than that, he has restored the reputation of the last squire, Sir Erasmus Griffies-Williams, the only member of the family until now remembered at all, because of the very amusing character assassination by H.M. Vaughan in his well-known The South Wales Squires (1926). Likewise the first baronet, of whom it had been suggested that his title was owed only to his friendship with the Prince Regent, is revealed as having solid worth. Certainly he was a man of culture, for the landscaped park that he had laid out at Llwynywermod was highly picturesque and sophisticated, fine enough still, after long abandonment, to be included on Cadw's Register of Landscapes, Parks and Gardens of Special Historic Interest.

By a wonderful coincidence, a large watercolour painting of the park and house, by one of Sir Erasmus's daughters, sold by a descendant in the late 1970s, turned up at a small auction near London a month before this book went to press and images are included here. Llwynywermod's fortunes are turning upward once again after a century of doldrums. The recent owners, John and Patricia Hegarty, unsung heroes, restored the ruined walled garden and fought to protect the fragile landscape from a monstrous pipeline's projected route. Now under its greatly welcomed new ownership, further very thoughtfully designed improvements have followed, which will allow many guests to have access to this beautiful domain. The old house may well be presently ruined but the spirit of this lovely place is no longer a memory but a reality.

Introduction

Following in the footsteps of Hafod Uchtryd, it comes as no surprise that Sir George Griffies-Williams and his wife, Anna Margaretta, set about creating a showpiece picturesque landscape at Llwynywormwood, Myddfai. William Gilpin's highly influential tour through parts of South Wales addresses Llandovery and its environs in terms of the picturesque ideal, as an area of unadulterated beauty whose natural appearance was most pleasing to the eye and could be viewed as if it were a painting. Gilpin describes Llandovery and the Towy Valley thus: 'the woodland views are more frequent, and the whole more wild and simple. The scenery seems precisely of that kind with which a great master in landscape was formerly enamoured.' [1] It was this publication, based upon a tour during the summer of 1770 that helped launch the picturesque movement and changed the way in which people viewed landscapes. Llwynywormwood lent itself naturally to the picturesque ideal; its undulating scenery falls and rises through hills, woodlands and streams towards the dramatic outline of Mynydd Myddfai and the Carmarthenshire Vans. A measure of subtlety and aptitude that was achieved by the designers not only managed to retain the wild sense of the country yet also to uphold all the elements of sophisticated parkland. The rich and

Fig. 4. *Sir Erasmus Griffies-Williams is perhaps one of the most famous owners of Llwynywormwood. He was a man of letters and an accomplished Welsh linguist, at the time of his sudden death he was working on a lexicon of Welsh into English, which unfortunately was never completed. Courtesy of the National Trust.*

---

[1] William Gilpin, <u>Observations on the River Wye</u>, (London: 1782) p. 102.

fertile soils of the Towy valley have enabled this area to be inhabited for thousands of years, with generation upon generation living, working and enjoying the varied beauties of the locality and its peace and seclusion. The mansion house of Llwynywormwood is situated on a secluded, rocky precipice: high above its landscaped park, it affording views which are both enchanting and breathtaking, mixing the rugged with the sublime.

Interestingly, the historic name Llwynywormwood is both a mixture of Welsh and English: 'llwyn' literally translates as 'bush' or 'grove', rendering 'wormwood grove' as the literal translation. However, early documents refer to the estate as 'Llynwermood' or 'Llwynywermod'; here 'llyn' translates as 'lake', with the appellation connoting 'wormwood

Fig. 5. *A reconstruction of the mansion house at Llwynywermod, recreated as it was during the early nineteenth century. Drawn by Ceri Leeder in 2007. See figure 84 to see how she came to piece together how the Plas once looked. Author's collection.*

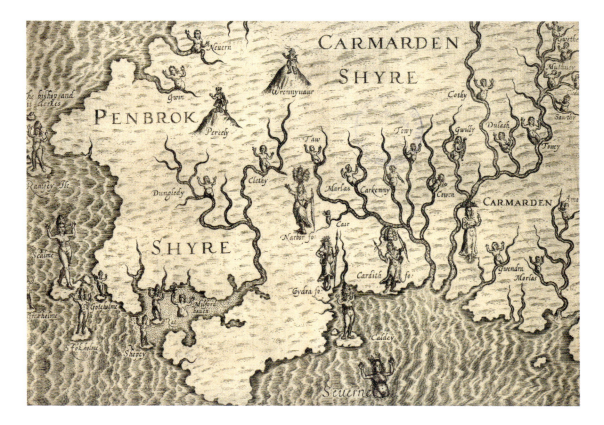

Fig. 6. *An early map of Carmarthenshire, dated to about the year 1600, showing the main rivers of the County. Llwynywermod is situated near to the village of Myddfai, spelt Muthvey in this instance, in the top right-hand corner. Courtesy of Cardiff University Archive.*

lake'. For the interests of historical accuracy, the form 'Llwynywormwood' has been used throughout this work until its purchase by the Duchy of Cornwall, when the name reverted to the more correct 'Llwynywermod'. Wormwood is a hardy perennial, native to Europe. It was believed to counteract poison as well as being a widely used disinfectant during the medieval period. Thomas Tusser during the mid-fifteenth century recorded that, in the mid-summer, wormwood was recommended for collecting and strewing, as was the practice of the day, about chambers and cupboards to keep away moths and insects:

During times of plague and pestilence, wormwood was worn or hung in rooms as it was a reliable flea repellent. Thomas Culpeper also wrote passionately about wormwood,

Fig. 7. Hafod retains one of Wales's most sophisticated designed landscapes, planned and laid out in a picturesque manner around the same time as Llwynywormwood was being developed by Sir George Griffies-Williams and his wives. Like Hafod, the mansion at Llwynywormwood served as the focal point for the pleasure walks and parkland planting. Author's collection.

'While wormwood hath seed, get handful or twaine,
To save against March to make flea to refraine;
Where chamber is sweeped, and wormwood is strowne
No flea for his life dar abide to be known.
What saver is better (if physicke be true)
For places infected, than wormwood and rue.
It is as a comfort for hart and the braine
And therefore to have it, it is not in vaine.'[2]

[2] Kay N. Sanecki, History of the English herb garden, (London: 1992), p. 39.

but its use in the making of absinth and vermouth is for what it is later well-known. Additionally, the essential oil of wormwood was in part infused with ale and beer to make purl and in Scotland it was similarly used by the distillers of whisky. [3]

According to Samuel Lewis's *Topographical Dictionary of Wales*, Myddfai was much frequented by physicians, amongst whom was a man known as Rhiwallon, who with his three sons distinguished himself with a manuscript treatise on the practice of physic.

Fig. 8. *This watercolour was sold in 1979 by the executors of the will of Amy Elizabeth Noon from her home in Truro. It was painted by her grandmother, Juliana Graves-Sawle in 1870 whilst on a visit to the estate before the sudden death of her father, Sir Erasmus Griffies-Williams. It is probably the only accurate contemporary image to survive showing the extensive park and mansion house during their prime. One can clearly see the white-washed mansion house rising magnificently above lake, whilst the carefully planted trees frame the perimeters. It is important to note that the planting of the central portion of the park appears to be principally deciduous broadleaf, while the outskirts are bordered with evergreen conifers and firs. It is understandable why Sir Erasmus in his will specifically forbade the felling of any trees in the estate's golden core. Courtesy of Thomas Lloyd.*

[3] Lesley Gordon, <u>A Country Herbal</u>, (London: 1980), p. 195.

And then to awake, and the farm, like a wanderer white with the dew, come back, the cock on his shoulder: it was all Shining, it was Adam and maiden, The sky gathered again And the sun grew round that very day. So it must have been after the birth of the simple light In the first, spinning place, the spellbound horses walking warm Out of the whinnying green stable On to the fields of praise — Dylan Thomas "Fern Hill"

with apologies to Nicholas Poussin

Fig. 9. *A panoramic architectural drawing by the Duchy of Cornwall architect Craig Hamilton, showing the farm and Mansion House beyond. Courtesy of Craig Hamilton Architects.*

Tradition asserts that his descendants continued to follow the practice of medicine in the parish till within living memory at the turn of the nineteenth century. [4] A sense of history and the importance of heritage has been recently captured by a locally organised team who recorded the memories of local people recalling stories of life in Myddfai during the last century. Many tales of herbal remedies and practices, some based upon age-old customs, were prevalent throughout, thus creating a tangible link with the famed

---

[4] Samuel Lewis, A Topographical Dictionary of Wales, (London, 1845), p. 246.
    First Published in 1822 and subsequently reprinted.

Physicians of Myddfai. Llwynywormwood played its part too; over a hundred years ago a book was purchased from the sale of contents of the mansion house by local historian Francis Green and contained within its leather-bound pages were hand-written transcriptions of legal precedents and medicinal and culinary recipes. [5] It has been dated to the late seventeenth or early eighteenth centuries, and seems to have originated from Carmarthen. It is entirely possible that it once formed part of the Williams family's library, which was still virtually intact in 1898 when the house contents were dispersed. Unfortunately, it cannot be discerned as to how the book found its way to Llwynywormwood but it seems probable that it passed into the hands of the family during the early eighteenth century.

---

[5] NLW MSS/4492D

Fig. 10. *One of the fireplaces in situ at Llwynywormwood in 1979. Compare to figure 76. Courtesy of RCAHMW.*

Llwynywormwood was at its height around the turn of the nineteenth century when a decisive series of improvements took place both at the mansion house itself and the surrounding parkland. The evolution of the medieval house had come into maturity with extensions and alterations by Sir George Griffies-Williams and his wives, to house his burgeoning young family. Llwynywormwood was typically Welsh, having its many changes on full view so that visitors could see the house's development over its several hundred years in existence. In stone and mortar one could see a family's fortune blossoming and receding, their changing tastes, thoughts and ideals, from the earliest extant genesis found in the medieval bakehouse through to the Georgian bell-tower which seems to have easily been extracted from an Irish round tower and a Victorian kitchen range which is a forlorn lone survivor amongst the ruins. In respect of this I have divided the book into two distinct sections: the first deals with, discusses and chronicles the families who have lived, loved and died at Llwynywormwood and the second focuses on the architectural points of the mansion, estate and landscape. Yet as the restoration continues, I am sure that many more secrets have yet to be yielded and which can only come forth as work continues on site. Therefore, this account is not exhaustive and can only shed light on what has been discovered to date; even as I am putting the finishing touches to this introduction, more facts and snippets of information keep springing up to add further colour and texture to the historical tapestry of narrative that forms the story behind any house and family, whether they be large or small, Tudor or Edwardian, country house or cottage.

This book was originally commissioned by the Welsh Historic Gardens Trust for presentation to TRH The Prince of Wales and The Duchess of Cornwall, to commemorate the historic purchase of the farm and estate as a base in Wales for Their Royal Highnesses and The Prince's Charities. Presentation of a handmade, leather-bound copy of the book took place during February 2008 at Llwynywormwood itself. Writing had begun in earnest back in October 2006 with virtually no previous research undertaken. The whole project from start to finish was virgin territory as there has been no other attempt to unravel the intricacies of this ancient Welsh estate. This in turn has made researching and writing this estate treatise a most pleasurable, rewarding and absorbing process, disentangling a somewhat complicated and convoluted history of a long forgotten family and their home, which had for over four hundred years been of substantial standing. Through the distortion of time, memory and misinterpreted facts, much of the previously published material proved to be inaccurate, thus this reinterpretation comes as doubly necessitated. It is hoped that this book will provide a clear and objective account of the evolution and fortunes of Llwynywormwood, to provide a background for its no doubt splendid and deserving future.

Mark Baker

GREIF · Y · FYDD

The Williams & Griffies-Williams of Llwynywormwood

Through ten generations, from Daniel Williams in the early seventeenth century, through to Amy Elizabeth (Elly) Prinn Noon, who died in 1979, the family which oversaw the flowering and subsequent decline of Llwynywormwood saw its fortunes rise and fall approximately in parallel with the estate.

The estate owners' changes of name from Williams, tracing its ancestry back to Norman times, to Griffies-Williams, to Graves-Sawle and to Prinn Noon speak of the early deaths, and lack of prolificacy, of male heirs which contributed to Llwynywormwood's descent into ruin.

The estate reached its peak in the time of Sir George Griffies-Williams and his wife, Anna Margaretta. Sir George fathered no fewer than five male and five female heirs. That there should have been no Griffies-Williamses to inherit, just two generations later, was as unforeseeable as was the collapse of the estate.

Sir George himself inherited only when David Williams's only son, Erasmus, died childless at the age of thirty-one. As well as acceding to the estate, he added 'Williams' to his name due to a conditional clause laid down in the will of David Williams who desired that the name would remain linked to Llwynywormwood in perpetuity. Alas, posterity has seen both the name die out and the estate fall into disuse.

Happily and fortuitously, the estate has now become the property of the Duchy of Cornwall, serving primarily as a Welsh base for HRH The Prince of Wales, and it is to be hoped that Llwynywormwood, now reverted in name to Llwynywermod, will now enjoy the prosperous future David Williams and his descendants undoubtedly foresaw for it.

Fig. 11. *A watercolour depicting the Coat of Arms for the Griffies-Williams Family. Arms – quarterly; 1st and 4th ar. on a chev. engr. gu. between 3 bulls heads, cabossed, sa. a rose between two fleurs-de-lis, of the field for Williams; 2nd & 3rd , a2; a fesse, dancette, erm. between four griffins, segreant, or, for Griffies. Compare with the bookplate in figure 23 and the needlework in figure 48. Courtesy of the National Trust.*

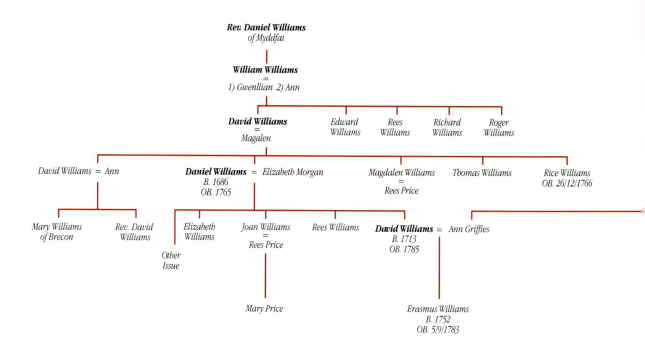

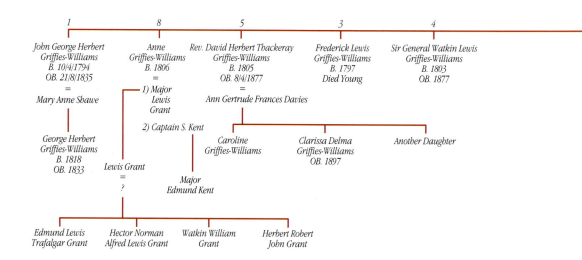

(bold) *Owners of Llwynywermod*

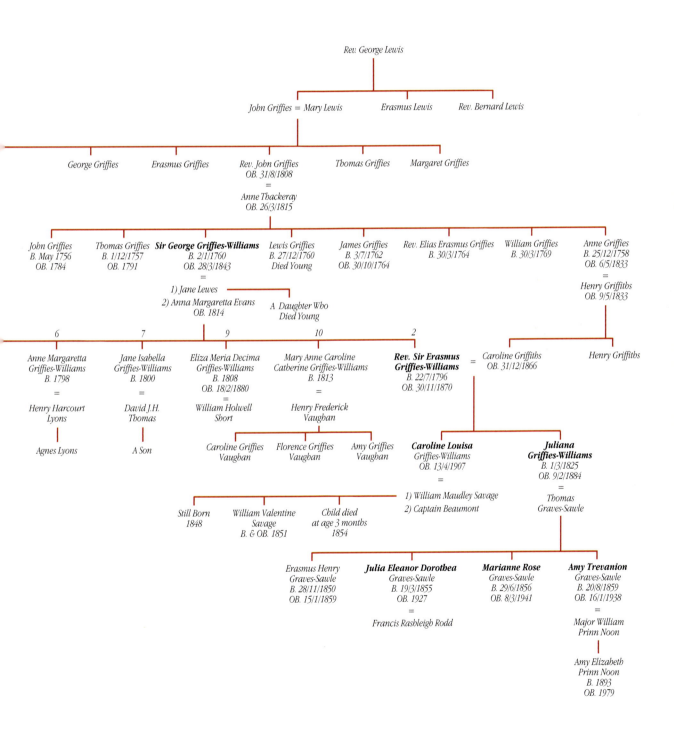

Rev. George Lewis

John Griffies = Mary Lewis   Erasmus Lewis   Rev. Bernard Lewis

George Griffies   Erasmus Griffies   Rev. John Griffies
OB. 31/8/1808
=
Anne Thackeray
OB. 26/3/1815
    Thomas Griffies   Margaret Griffies

John Griffies
B. May 1756
OB. 1784

Thomas Griffies
B. 1/12/1757
OB. 1791

Sir George Griffies-Williams
B. 2/1/1760
OB. 28/3/1843
=
1) Jane Lewes
2) Anna Margaretta Evans
OB. 1814

Lewis Griffies
B. 27/12/1760
Died Young

A Daughter Who
Died Young

James Griffies
B. 3/7/1762
OB. 30/10/1764

Rev. Elias Erasmus Griffies
B. 30/3/1764

William Griffies
B. 30/3/1769

Anne Griffies
B. 25/12/1758
OB. 6/5/1833
=
Henry Griffiths
OB. 9/5/1833

6   **7**   **9**   **10**   **2**

Anne Margaretta
Griffies-Williams
B. 1798
=
Henry Harcourt
Lyons

Jane Isabella
Griffies-Williams
B. 1800
=
David J.H.
Thomas

Eliza Meria Decima
Griffies-Williams
B. 1808
OB. 18/2/1880
=
William Holwell
Short

Mary Anne Caroline
Catherine Griffies-Williams
B. 1813
=
Henry Frederick
Vaughan

Rev. Sir Erasmus
Griffies-Williams
B. 22/7/1796
OB. 30/11/1870
= Caroline Griffiths
OB. 31/12/1866

Henry Griffiths

Agnes Lyons

A Son

Caroline Griffies
Vaughan

Florence Griffies
Vaughan

Amy Griffies
Vaughan

Caroline Louisa
Griffies-Williams
OB. 13/4/1907
=
1) William Maudley Savage
2) Captain Beaumont

Juliana
Griffies-Williams
B. 1/3/1825
OB. 9/2/1884
=
Thomas
Graves-Sawle

Still Born
1848

William Valentine
Savage
B. & OB. 1851

Child died
at age 3 months
1854

Erasmus Henry
Graves-Sawle
B. 28/11/1850
OB. 15/1/1859

Julia Eleanor Dorothea
Graves-Sawle
B. 19/3/1855
OB. 1927
=
Francis Rashleigh Rodd

Marianne Rose
Graves-Sawle
B. 29/6/1856
OB. 8/3/1941

Amy Trevanion
Graves-Sawle
B. 20/8/1859
OB. 16/1/1938
=
Major William
Prinn Noon

Amy Elizabeth
Prinn Noon
B. 1893
OB. 1979

Early History & The Williams Family

Before the coming of the Normans, Wales was administered territorially by division into Cantrefi, these in turn were subdivided into areas called Cymydau or commotes. Llwynywormwood was situated in the Cantref Bychan, which was administered in three commotes; Hirfryn, Perfedd and Is Cennen. Perfedd was partitioned into four maenors of which Myddfai was one. William Rees states that this was characteristic of the southern bank of the River Towy and that the maenors were occupied by Welsh freemen varying in number from forty to one hundred. [6] In 1116, Cantref Bychan was invaded by the Anglo-Norman forces from Brecon under the leadership of Richard Fitz Pons, who consequently established a castle at Llandovery. [7] The whole region was acquired by the Clifford Lords of Brecon, under the auspices of the 'Lordship of Llandovery'. Their hold was particularly tenuous as between 1154 and 1163 the lordship was transferred several times back and forth to the famous native Welsh leader, Rhys ap Gruffydd. King Henry II whilst in a weak position latterly granted Rhys the right to rule as a Lord the ancient Welsh kingdom of Deheubarth, which included the strategic locations of Llandovery and Carmarthen. [8]

Fig. 12. *It is from Abercamlais near Brecon, that the Williams family of Llwynywormwood were directly descended. Author's collection.*

[6] William Rees, South Wales and the March: 1284 – 1415, (Oxford: 1924), p. 203.
[7] William Rees, An historical atlas of Wales from early to modern times, (Cardiff, 1951), p. 29.
[8] Ibid., p. 33.

Fig. 13. *Llandovery Castle was established by Richard Fitz Pons following the invasion of Cantref Bychan in 1116. The local area which included Llwynywormwood would have been administered from the castle at Llandovery. Author's collection.*

Under Llewellyn the Great, Cantref Bychan was governed by his loyal subjects during the early thirteenth century. After Llewellyn's death in 1240, his son Dafydd succeeded to the overlordship, but lacked the strength of his father and was killed during battle in 1246 at Garth Celyn. The 'Treaty of Woodstock' a year later saw the rulers of Deheubarth switch their allegiance to the English monarch. Llewellyn the Great's grandson, Llewellyn ap Gruffydd, retook Cantref Bychan where Maredudd, son of Rhys Gryg, recognised him as overlord in 1270. Rhys Gryg 'held the castle of Llandovery with the commotes of Perfedd and Hirfryn, in his demesne as of fee, from Llewellyn ap Gruffydd, formerly Prince of Wales, by Welsh services and customs.' [9] These lands had been passed by the heirs male right down to Rhys' great grandsons who possessed as a consequence the positions of Barons or Lords of Wales. [10]

---

[8] Ibid., p. 33.   [9] Rees, <u>South Wales and the March</u>, p. 22.   [10] Ibid.

One of the earliest mentions of St Michael's Church, Myddfai comes from 1284 when the advowson fell to Edward I. [11] It is likely that the church was dedicated prior to the Norman Conquest and that there may have been an early medieval Christian site in the vicinity as Talley Abbey owned much of the surrounding land. Maenor Myddfai became a manor under the English model following Llandovery's fall to English forces in 1277 when Maredudd defected. [12] A still visible moated site of medieval date was constructed a few

Fig. 14. *Llanfihangel ym Myddfai as seen from the main gates. It was at the parish church in Myddfai that the Reverend Daniel Williams was installed as Vicar and it has been suggested that Llwynywormwood served as his residence. During the early nineteenth century, the Llwynywormwood Estate was allocated by the church eight rows of pews for its tenants. Each pew contained sixteen seats, giving a total of 128. Author's collection.*

---

[11] The advowson was subsequently passed to the Bishop of St Davids.
[12] Llandovery was assailed once again by Welsh militia in 1282 during the second War of Independence

hundred yards to the south of St Michael's, suggesting that there was already some substantial settlement in the vicinity. [13] This moated site could well have been the centre from which the manor of Myddfai was directly administered.

Under the Statute of Rhuddlan in 1284, Llandovery and the Cantref Bychan were assimilated into the Lordship of Carmarthen and Cardigan, with John Giffard as Lord of Llandovery. Carmarthenshire County was thus in due course created by an arbitrary grouping of Lordships which had been perpetuated by the ancient Cantrefi. [14] The fourteenth century with its plagues and fluctuations in populations was a relatively stable

Fig. 15. *A recent photograph of the medieval fireplace in the bakehouse range. It was very common for kitchens to be detached from the main house during the Middle Ages to reduce the risk of the spread of fire. Author's collection.*

---

[13] Discovered relatively recently, this square earthwork measures approximately 50m by 60m, consisting of an outer moat with a level inner platform. Some 360m to the south-west lies another moated site, Castell Waunberllan.

[14] Rees, <u>Historical Atlas of Wales</u>, p. 53.

Fig. 16. *The detached kitchen, latterly used as a bakehouse, is the earliest surviving section of the 'Plas' at Llwynywormwood. Its survival is based chiefly upon its reuse during the late twentieth century as a cow shed which meant that the roof was kept in relatively good condition. Courtesy of the RCAHMW.*

period; it was Owain Glyndwr's rebellion in 1400, when Llandovery was under the control of the Audleys, that broke this stability. [15] The Acts of Union of 1536 and 1542 united Wales with England, introducing the English style of administration throughout the country. Each shire was then divided up into hundreds as in England, which came under the jurisdiction of Justices of the Peace who held Petty Sessions of the Hundred where 'minor cases were tried and local affairs transacted.' [16]

It was during the early seventeenth century that the Williams family were first mentioned in connection with Llwynywormwood; Daniel Williams of Abercamlais, Brecon was Vicar of Myddfai and Llanspyddid and had married Sarah, daughter of John Lewis of Ffrwdgrech, Brecon. The Williamses were able to trace their ancestry right back to the eleventh century. Thomas Nicolas describes how the Norman knight, Bernard de Neuf Marché, or Newmarch conquered the area known as Brycheiniog, now Breconshire. Amongst the companion knights of Bernard was one who had probably come from the neighbourhood of Boulogne, for he went by the name *de Boulogne* or Bullen and it is from him that all of the Williamses and their collateral branches were descended. A famous descendent of this knight was Henry VIII's tragic queen, Anne Boleyn, mother of Queen Elizabeth I.

---

[15] During the Wars of the Roses, the Cantref Bychan was held by Lancastrian supporters.
[16] Ibid., p. 55.

Fig. 17. *Pont Dolauhirion, near Llandovery, is an unusual single arched bridge, similar in construction to the two bridges found at Llwynywormwood Park. This highly romanticised engraving seems more akin to Tuscany rather than Carmarthenshire. Author's collection.*

Reverend Daniel Williams had two sons, Thomas, the eldest inherited Abercamlais,[17] and William, who settled at Llwynywormwood, which may have previously served as the Vicar of Myddfai's residence. William is recorded to have married, firstly, Gwenllian and had five sons, David, Edward, Rees, Richard and Roger, all of whom were born following the Civil War. The family had fought for the Royalist cause and were thus forced to pay penalties under Acts of Parliament that were passed in 1648 and 1649 for South and North Wales respectively. However, since it was particularly difficult to apply this policy in Wales, set amounts were raised for each county; Carmarthenshire was fined £4,000 and William Williams himself was penalised £100 for being a defeated Cavalier who had given assistance to the King. [18]

---

[17] Thomas' sons, John and Richard, became respectively founders of the branch families of Penpont and Aberbrân.
[18] Sir John E. Lloyd, A history of Carmarthenshire Vol. II, (Cardiff, 1935).

After Gwenllian's death, William Williams married Ann with whom he had no children. She was still alive in 1694 when Edward Williams challenged the last will and testament and estate of his father, particularly in respect of a lease granted by his brother David of several parcels of land situated in Myddfai. David Williams had inherited Llwynywormwood and married Magdalen; they had five children; Daniel, Thomas, Rees, Magdalen and David. It was their first son Daniel, born in 1686, who inherited the Llwynywormwood estate. He subsequently married Elizabeth Morgan and together they had six children: David, Margaret, Rees, John, Elizabeth and Mary. Our only reference to Daniel's life and work is a mention that he was duly elected as a Burgess of the County of Carmarthen on 2nd October 1738, together with his son, David. [19] This indicates that the family were recognised and of standing during the early eighteenth century.

David Williams the second was born in 1713 and baptised at Myddfai Church; he became an attorney at law and had his business premises at the Green Post, King Street, Carmarthen. David married Anne Griffies, daughter of John Griffies of Coed, Llandyfaelog, in 1751. Only one child survived, Erasmus Williams, born in 1752. On 25th July 1757, David Williams was sworn into the Common Council of the County Borough of Carmarthen, from which he resigned on 3rd October but was shortly re-elected. [20] David was said to be good friends with the notorious Sir Herbert Lloyd of Peterwell, Lampeter and in 1761 they both lived for a while together at Tunbridge Wells, for their health's sake. A letter survives from Sir Herbert which states that '...*David Williams, the attorney of Carmarthen (who lives with me)...came ill here 3 weeks ago, and is greatly recovered and out of danger now, and will return to me to Wales.*' [21]

The following letter extract was written to Erasmus Williams whilst at King Street, Carmarthen. It had been transcribed by George Eyre Evans in 1917 from a compiled collection of bound letters, put together for protection in the form of a book. The 'letter-book' was at this time in the ownership of Mrs Jones of Ysgubor Fawr, Penderyn, Glamorgan. One of the most interesting of the letters was from John Griffies and written on 28th January 1780 – '*Many thanks to my good cousin for his last kind favour, but am very sorry to find his poor father has got a return of his old complaint – low spirits, the most pitiable malady any man can have, but as air and exercise is the best and indeed only remedy. I would recommend him a little recreation of coursing up at*

---

[19] Carmarthenshire Antiquarian Society Transactions, Vol. 3, p. 3.
[20] Ibid., Vol. 1, p. 95.   [21] Ibid., Vol. 3, p. 3.

Llanpumpsant, where he may at the same time have the satisfaction (a very great one) of having served his brother very specially, by obliging my tenants there to do us common justice, and pay in immediately one year's rent at least for two are due…'

Very much a part of the community and local society, Erasmus was affectionately nicknamed 'Muss' or 'Mussy' by his friends and family. For several years he would preach the sermons at Llangunnor Church on Ash Wednesday and Good Friday, pursuant to the will of a Mrs Pardoe. Sadly this happy state of affairs was not to last and a letter from the Cwmgwili collection mentions a meeting with both David and Erasmus Williams, where Erasmus was said to have looked 'like death'. [22] Erasmus, probably sensing his demise, made out his Last Will and Testament on 17th April 1783, leaving all of his real and personal estate to his father who was also his sole executor. [23]

'In this sacred place.
Let the name of ERASMUS WILLIAMS be preserved.
His virtues and integrity are still lamented by
all who knew him
and had he lived he would have enjoyed an ample fortune
but he was cut off in the 32nd year of his age
on the 5th September 1783
and left an aged father whose sorrows knew no end
until he rested in the adjoining grave.
He was the only son of David Williams late of Llwynywormwood
in this parish Esq by Anne his wife daughter of
John Griffies late of Coed in this county Esqr.
This monument was erected agreeable to the
directions of the Will of his affectionate father.'

Inscription from memorial tablet at Myddfai Church. [24]

---

[22] CRO/Cwmgwili/Miss/II/761 Pg. 347: 21st June 1783?   [23] PRO/Prob/11/1128 – Image ref. 92.
[24] Richard Fenton's Tours in Wales, 1809, is very complimentary about the memorial tablet, particularly noting its expense.

Fig. 18. *A photograph of the memorial tablet to Erasmus Williams in the parish church at Myddfai, sadly the lettering today is virtually indiscernible and is in need of restoration. Such a fine and expensive sepulchral monument clearly displays the wealth and aspiration, as well as admiration shown by Sir George Griffies-Williams who erected the tablet. Author's collection.*

Fig. 19. *This miniature was passed down through the Williams and Griffies-Williams families for several generations. It is thought to show Daniel Williams (1686 – 1765) or his son David Williams (1713 – 1785). Courtesy of the Noon Collection.*

Another insight into the period comes from Mrs Anne Philipps of Cwmgwili who frequently wrote to her M.P. husband regarding matters in Carmarthenshire. Incidentally one of the frequent topics was David Williams of Llwynywormwood. '...Mr Griffies of Coyd's brother is going to law with him, to dispute Mr Davy Williams's will, so that in all probability what was got by slander and cheating will be spent on law.' [25] This epithet is rather ambiguous as to whom the 'slander and cheating' refers to. Could it be that Mr Griffies had influenced Davy Williams to alter his will, diminishing the share of his brother?

A month later she goes on to write '...*Mr Davy Williams is very ill, he is given over by Doctor Davies, his complaint is a frensy on the Brain, all owing to his drinking brandy. If anything should happen to him, don't forget to secure the tithe from Lady Dynevor.*' [26] A fragment of a letter survives which states that '...*Mr Davy Williams who has been dying for this last week and given out by all who saw him is now much better and in a fair way of recovery, but the Doctor says that his recovery depends all upon himself. He drank the week before he fell ill three bottles of brandy every day. He was in convulsion fits all day last Monday.*' [27]

David Williams the second died at the end of April, 1785, a depressed and lonely man following the death of Erasmus. There was no direct heir, so the estate was bequeathed to his nephew. His legacy however was still felt in 1906 when a vast collection of documents was discovered stored away in a room at Llwynywormwood, untouched since his death some one hundred and twenty years earlier. Some of the documents dated back as far as the fifteenth century and many related to some of the principal South Wales families. The bulk of them were title deeds and many were in Latin; regrettably, their present location is unknown. [28]

[25] CRO/Cwmgwili/Miss/II/186 Pg. 95: 23rd February 1785.   [26] CRO/Cwmgwili/Miss/II/203 Pg. 106: 23rd April 1785.
[27] CRO/Cwmgwili/Miss/II/709 Pg. 358.   [28] *The Western Mail*, 31st March 1906.

Sir George Griffies-Williams
1785 ~ 1843

Llwynywormwood, together with a small fortune, was bequeathed to David Williams' twenty-five-year-old Eton-educated nephew, George Griffies, third son of Reverend John and Ann Griffies. He wrote from Brecon on 2nd May 1785 to the solicitors in Llandovery, 'acquainting' himself with them as he was planning to visit. [29] One of the conditions of David Williams' inheritance was that George would additionally assume his surname. [30] This was done by Sign Manual on 21st May 1785 and thus George Griffies-Williams took up residence at Llwynywormwood. Farming was an important part of the ethos with which George managed the estates, and by August he was already negotiating the purchase of hay from Abercothy, together with a wagon and four large black Herefordshire horses. [31] Meanwhile, George continued with his studies at St John's College, Cambridge and graduated with his Master of Arts in 1786.

Fig. 20. *A portrait possibly of Sir George Griffies-Williams (1760 – 1843), circa 1830s by an unknown artist. It shows Sir George seated with a snuff box in one hand and on the nearby table, a magnifying glass standing next to what looks like a newspaper. Courtesy of the National Trust.*

---

[29] NLW/D.T.M.Jones/8076. 2nd May 1785.
[30] PRO/Prob/11/1128 – Image ref. 93.
[31] NLW/D.T.M.Jones/8080.

Fig. 21. *Jane Lewes was the first wife of Sir George Griffies-Williams and died shortly after giving birth to a daughter at Llwynywormwood. The Evans family hailed from Pembrokeshire but her uncle had meteorically risen to become Sir Watkin Lewes, Lord Mayor of London. Courtesy of the Noon Collection.*

By this time he had firmly settled himself into life at Llwynywormwood, dining with members of the local gentry, including Mr Rice of Llwynybrain, frequently visiting Bath and hunting with friends and neighbours. [32] The Society for the Encouragement of Arts, Manufactures and Commerce elected George as a member during 1787. [33] This is a very notable achievement, indicating that George was indeed an excellent farmer and landowner. Estate matters were also of great importance, and George showed himself to be a conscientious and 'polite' gentleman, who took his position in society in earnest.

[32] Ibid. 8145.
[33] *The Times*, Friday, June 8th 1787.

Fig. 22. *Half-length oil portrait of Anna Margaretta Griffies-Williams which once hung at Llwynywormwood, circa 1790s by an unknown artist.* 'Her sash is scarlet, as is the ribbon in her hair which is powdered and profusely curled.' *Courtesy of the National Trust.*

When a property called Erryd became problematic concerning the whereabouts of the deeds, George, who had them stored at Carmarthen, went there himself from Llwynywormwood to recover the documents. [34]

In the meantime, George had married Jane, sole heiress of Reverend John Lewes of Tredefaid, Pembrokeshire and niece of Sir Watkin Lewes, Lord Mayor of London. George fathered a daughter with Jane, who sadly died shortly after her mother at a tender young age, leaving a doubly grieving husband and father behind. It may have been due to her

[34] NLW/D.T.M.Jones/8197.

influence that a town coach or chariot was ordered on 29th April 1789 from Messrs Windus and Son of London – *'To a new chariot made of the best material and very sound workmanship neatly carved and painted dark blue with ciphers and crest enclosed in circle painted on all panels lined with a fine buff cloth and trimmed with… spotted lace, blue and buff broad lace… and holders, falls of seat best Wilton carpet, best plate glasses and inside trunk the body covered with the best japanned leather, hung upon a fashionable strait perch carriage with lofty town made steel springs, iron covered cross trees, platform boat, high coach box made to take off occasionally, the carriage painted red and varnished vermillion and neatly picked two colours blue and buff, crest painted on foot board with a handsome full gathered seat cloth trimmed with three rows of handsome gimp fringe and two rows of double broad spotted lace.'* [35] The total cost was £149 – 4s 6d. So important was the chariot that a separate ledger was kept specifically for the town coach; various alterations, cleanings and repairs were meticulously recorded for several years. An example of this was on 15th May 1789 when a new strong travelling trunk covered with leather and lined with cotton was purchased to be placed on the rear of the coach. [36]

A further honour for George came in his appointment as High Sheriff of Carmarthenshire for the year 1791. [37] Through his new position, George was often in Carmarthen itself, and also at Highmead, which was the home of his future second wife. Following the death of Jane, George married Anna Margaretta, daughter of Herbert Evans Esq., of Highmead, Cardiganshire, who was twenty-one years old when they married at Llanwenog church with the consent of her mother, Anne Evans. During October 1791, Anna Margaretta was gravely ill at Llwynywormwood, so unwell in fact that all visitors to the house were turned away until she had recovered. George wrote that 'we have a sick house at present' but he hoped to receive guests again as soon as was convenient. [38] Around two months later Anna Margaretta had recovered sufficiently for visitors to return once more to Llwynywormwood, with George offering the 'compliments of the season' to his friends. [39] Anna Margaretta and George embarked on improving the estate and buying furniture for the house; various receipts have survived from 1792, the year in which it may be surmised that Llwynywormwood was altered and extended.

The newly wedded couple, in a state of domestic felicity, purchased from Willows &

[35] CRO/CAS/ix, pp. 1 – 13.   [36] Ibid.
[37] Thomas Nicolas, Annals and Antiquities of the Counties and County Families of Wales, (London: 1872), p. 276.
[38] NLW/D.T.M.Jones/8673.   [39] Ibid. 8703.

GREIF Y FYDD

Fig. 23. *A bookplate depicting the arms of Sir George Griffies-Williams. The library at Llwynywormwood was said to be extensive and contained many old and valuable manuscripts, some even dating back to the fifteenth century. Courtesy of Thomas Lloyd.*

Fig. 24. *Mary Anne Evans of Highmead, Llanybydder, sister to Anna Margaretta Evans, wife of Sir George Griffies-Williams. Mary Anne married Walter Rice of Llwynybrain, near Llandovery and this portrait now hangs at Dynevor Park, Llandeilo. Courtesy of the National Trust.*

Warren of London '...*one Brussels carpet ... twenty-two yards Brussels stair carpets, thirty brass rods & staples, a turkey carpet twenty-two foot by thirteen foot six inches, a Kidd carpet, three pile rugs, one six foot bed bolster, two down pillows eight feet long, one six foot hair mattress... total £94 2 7.'* All were sent by parcel from London to Llwynywormwood. '*George Simson, upholder, cabinet-maker and undertaker – May 16th 1792 – one pair of fine black rosewood card tables, richly inlaid, lined and highly varnished. One Pembroke table to match on castors. Denmark leather covers to match. Two carved and gilt bracket plates. One very long cove window cornice with tablet in centre, to join richly.'* A few days later on 19th May, '*three yellow Stormont window curtains lined with fine white Calicoe to draw on pulley rods...'* were purchased together with two cove cornices for the dining parlour to match a long one previously bought.

From Thomas Barnard, a working goldsmith and jeweller in London, a new silver tea kettle lamp and coffee pot to match were procured. Furthermore, Barnard was commissioned to engrave the arms and crests of the Griffies-Williams on the silverware. E. Clark, Hardwareman and Silversmith of London, sold Pontypool ware to the Griffies-Williams; these included two pairs of chamber candlesticks, one sugar canister, two pairs of wax reels and one spice box. Anna Margaretta paid this bill herself and signed for it on 10th March 1792. Eleven days later more items from Clark were obtained; a Pontypool canister, four silver mounted forks, two silver ladles, two dozen best green ivory knives and forks with steel blades, and one pair of carvers with a guard fork.

Anna Margaretta's portrait shows her in the height of her beauty, dressed in white muslin, closing at the throat. Her sash is scarlet, as is the ribbon in her hair which is powdered and profusely curled. The portrait doubtlessly hung on one of the walls at Llwynywormwood and it has been suggested that she is shown sitting beneath one of her favourite trees on the estate. George and she had a total of ten children all born at Llwynywormwood and baptised at Myddfai; John George Herbert in 1794, Erasmus Henry in 1796, Frederick Lewis in 1797 who died young, Anna Margaretta in 1798, Jane Isabella in 1800, Watkin Lewis in 1803, David Herbert Thackeray in 1805, Anne in 1806, Eliza Maria Decima in 1808 and Mary Anne Caroline Catherine in 1813.

On 14th October 1796, George together with Jones Llwyd made a complaint in the Common Hall in Carmarthen against David Rees, one of the Common Councilmen. They

Fig. 25. *Said to be a brother of Sir George Griffies-Williams, possibly John Griffies (1756 – 1784). John was good friends with David and his son, Erasmus Williams, who frequently stayed with their Griffies cousins at Brecon. Courtesy of the Noon Collection.*

Fig. 26. *The earliest likeness of Anne Griffies (1758 – 1833) as a young woman, circa 1780. Courtesy of the Noon Collection.*

stated that on 5th October 1795, Rees had taken possession of the book in which orders were entered for the admission of ex-gratia Burgesses, and had on his own initiative ordered nine names to be entered into the book as Burgesses. Rees was subsequently turned out of his office and the vacant place in the Council was given to John Vaughan of Golden Grove. [40]   Representing the Whigs, George himself was elected one of the Councilmen for Carmarthen during September 1800. [41]

---

[40] Lloyd, <u>History of Carms.</u>, p.54.
[41] Ibid., p. 55.

Fig. 27. *A drawing of Henry Griffiths, husband of Anne Griffies, as a young man. Companion piece to figure 28. Courtesy of the Noon Collection.*

Fig. 28. *Anne Griffies (1758 – 1833) was the elder sister of Sir George Griffies-Williams and a renowned beauty who moved in the Court Circle of King George III and Queen Charlotte. This drawing is a companion piece to that of her husband, Henry Griffiths, and was probably commissioned to celebrate their marriage. Courtesy of the Noon Collection.*

In 1809 Richard Fenton, the Pembrokeshire historian and topographer published an account of a visit to Llwynywormwood from his Tour of Wales. He described the estate thus '...*a charming situation, ground very parkish, ornamented with fine masses of old wood. To the back a noble view of the mountains, which from hence look like the view of Cader Idris softened and in miniature from Dolgelly. Follow a narrow winding vale, each side well wooded, with a rippling stream passing through, dammed up into a large*

Fig. 29. *Anne Griffies, older sister of Sir George Griffies-Williams, and mother of Caroline Griffiths, a fine portrait which once hung at Llwynywormwood as a pair with figure 30. Courtesy of the National Trust.*

Fig. 30. *A portrait of Henry Griffiths, father of Caroline Griffiths and husband of Anne Griffies. Courtesy of the National Trust.*

pond under Llwynywormwood house, down to Cilgwyn…' [42] Fenton seems to have been one of the few diarists to have visited Llwynywormwood and recorded his observations, providing an albeit brief but very significant insight into the estate at this time.

In the county, during the late eighteenth and early nineteenth centuries, there were many political wrangles and intrigues between the Whigs and Tories, reaching a dramatic climax during the Carmarthen Mayoral elections of 1813 when George was elected Mayor. His main opponent was the Tory, D. J. Edwards of Rhyd y Gors who had been elected by his party to be Mayor. However, on the same day, at a later meeting, George was also elected to the position of Mayor. Edwards appealed to the King's Bench for a writ of *Quo Warranto* against George, in order to overturn his election. The court decided that, although the previous Mayor, David Morris had been in the meeting when Edwards was elected, he was not however presiding, therefore making the election invalid. [43] George was thus Mayor of Carmarthen in 1814.

George and Anna Margaretta both accompanied their son Erasmus to Cambridge [44] when he first went up to University there in 1814. Whilst staying at the hotel she was taken ill with a cold and also suffered inflammation. The doctors ordered her to be bled; Anna Margaretta herself strongly objected to this, exclaiming to those around 'will you stand by and see me murdered?' The doctors' will prevailed, but as soon as it was over, she turned her head on her pillow and died. [45] Naturally, George was overwhelmed with despair at his loss and he arranged for her body to be brought back to Wales for burial. The funeral was grand and filled with pomp; even the relations back in Cambridge were sent several black satin scarves and hatbands. It was remarked that this was a peculiarly Welsh custom. [46] Anna was described as a clever and spirited woman who was the stalwart of the family. Her descendants stated that as long as she lived all went well, but, after her death, Llwynywormwood was neglected, mortgages were raised and the family soon lost its once prominent local standing.

On 22nd May 1815, George Griffies-Williams was created a Baronet, a rare and uncommon event in Wales; however it was later questioned as to why he had been given such an honour. Did George "buy" his baronetcy in some underhand way or was he really friends with the Prince Regent? There is little evidence to suggest he was a personal friend of the Prince, except that he had been aligned with the Prince's political party, the Whigs,

---

[42] Richard Fenton, (John Fisher Eds.), Tours in Wales – 1804 – 1813. (London, 1917), pp. 73 – 74.   [43] Ibid. pp. 61 – 62.
[44] The family already had relatives living in Cambridge so this may have influenced their decision.
[45] Alicia Bayne & Jane Townley Pryme, Memorials of the Thackeray family, (London, 1879), p. 30.   [46] Ibid. p. 31.

Fig. 31 & 32. *A child's copy of figure 29 and figure 30 showing Anne Griffies and her husband, Henry Griffiths in old age. They were painted probably for practice by one of the children of Erasmus Griffies-Williams and were kept in pride of place on display in expensive frames at Llwynywormwood by Lady Caroline Griffies-Williams. Courtesy of the Noon Collection.*

for many years, and George had led them to prominence in the county. This in turn, may have been brought to the attention of the Prince via one of George's influential friends. More bizarrely, many years later a directory of coats of arms stated that proof was required of the legal creation of the Baronetcy, with the consequent right to inherit being put into jeopardy if this was not forthcoming. It is unclear whether proof was given as the Baronetcy had died out by this point. [47] Two weeks before his title was conferred, George was presented Burgess of Lampeter at the adjourned Court Leet, held in the Black Lion Inn on 4th May 1815.

[47] A. C. Fox-Davies, <u>Armorial families: A directory of some gentlemen of coat-armour, showing which arms in use at the moment are borne by legal authority,</u> (Edinburgh: 1898), p. 929.

All of these pretty miniatures are of members of the Griffies and Griffies-Williams families. However, their names have not been passed down and we cannot identify the sitters. Figures 33 and 35 may well be the same woman in youth and middle age. Courtesy of the Noon Collection.

Fig. 33.

Fig. 34.

Fig. 35.

Fig. 36. *Henry Griffiths Junior, son of Anne Griffies and Henry Griffiths, brother of Caroline Griffiths who married her first cousin, Erasmus Griffies-Williams. Courtesy of the Noon Collection.*

In 1825 Sir George became a director of the South Wales Mining Company, a business venture which may or may not have been rewarding. [48] He also continued as a Councillor for Carmarthen and it was in October 1833 that the State of the Carmarthen Corporation was inquired into and George was duly listed as being present and aged seventy-six. [49] The family were well known locally for benevolence and when a school was kept in Myddfai during the 1830s; Sir George paid for the fees of a number of children of the poor. [50] An estate sale took place in 1835 at the King's Head, Myddfai where three

---

[48] *The Times*, 30th March 1825.
[49] Carms. Society, V, pp. 74 – 75.
[50] Francis Jones, Historic Carmarthenshire homes and their families. (Carmarthen, 1987), p.122.

Fig. 37. *The Coat of Arms of John George Griffies-Williams (1794 – 1835), enamelled on the reverse of a memorial locket for his son, George Herbert (1818 – 1833). Courtesy of the Noon Collection.*

Fig. 38. *George Herbert Griffies-Williams's lock of hair, preserved in a gold locket, which also contains his miniature portrait (see figure 39) and a fine enamel displaying the Griffies-Williams Coat of Arms. The inscription reads 'Gge. Herbert Griffies Williams. Ob. June 15th 1833. Oetat: 15 years, 5 months and 21 days.' Courtesy of the Noon Collection.*

thousand oak and timber trees from the Llwynywormwood estate were to be sold. Those wishing to view the timber would be allowed to do so by the various occupying tenants. Was the estate perhaps slowly falling into debt at this stage or could this have been normal woodland management? Probably not, in light of the quantity involved.

Tragedy struck again on August 21st 1835 when Sir George's eldest son John George Herbert Griffies-Williams died at Boulogne, aged forty-one, leaving no surviving children,

Fig. 39. *George Herbert Griffies-Williams (1818 – 1833) was the first born grandchild of Sir George Griffies-Williams and only son of John George Griffies-Williams (1794 – 1835). He was a lively and clever young boy who was sent abroad to be educated. Courtesy of the Noon Collection.*

as his son George Herbert, who had been born in 1819, had died before him.[51] John had been married on 4th June 1816 to Mary Anne Shawe of Bath and for some time during the late 1820s was in residence at Llwynywormwood.[52] As the heir to Sir George, his death was a devastating blow to a rather fragile and elderly man. The heir to the Llwynywormwood estates was then Erasmus, the second son. Despite being close to his father, politically he and Sir George were diametrically opposed; Erasmus an ardent Tory

---

[51] PRO/Prob/11/1854 – Image ref. 293.
[52] The Gentleman's Magazine, 1835, p. 446.

Fig. 40. *A drawing of Llwynywormwood by an unknown artist dated 1812 or 1815, entitled* 'Llwynywormwood seat of G G Williams Carmarthenshire'. *What is most unusual about the house is the cupola at the top of the bell tower. Courtesy of the National Library of Wales.*

and his father a Whig. A family member recollected them both 'posting together with four horses from Wales to vote at a university election at Cambridge, and Sir George laughingly remarked…that they could not trust each other sufficiently to pair off.' [53] Later on in life, Sir George Griffies-Williams married for a third time, to Charlotte, some say that she was his cook with whom he is supposed to have had two children. There is only one piece of evidence to support the claims to her occupation, in the form of a note scribbled onto a

[53] Bayne & Pryme, Thackeray family, p. 31.

handwritten family tree for Llwynywormwood. [54] Lady Charlotte Griffies-Williams is a rather shadowy figure, who was thirty years George's junior yet predeceased him during late March 1840 at the age of forty-eight. [55]

In 1742, at the time of David Williams the third, the Llwynywormwood estate held twenty-three properties and contributed 13.5% of the chief-rent paid for the parish. [56] By 1839, the Llwynywormwood estate had grown to thirty-one properties and so owned 14.3% of the enclosed land in the parish, being the second largest after Cilgwyn. [57] It is remarkable that in one hundred years the estate had expanded so little, despite the family's rise in fortunes during the late eighteenth century.

Evidence is rather sparse for the later years of Sir George's life; it seems that Erasmus took up residence at some point during the late 1830s but this was probably on a sporadic basis. The 1841 census shows that there were four servants present at Llwynywormwood on the night the information was collected; these included the seventy-six year old Mary Rowland, her daughter Elizabeth Rowland, Elizabeth Griffiths and the nine-year-old Elizabeth Williams. Sir George died on 28th March 1843 at his London residence, 73 Albany Street, Regents Park, at the age of eighty-three and was buried in the catacombs at Kensal Green.

It is entirely possible that it was the influence of George's first two wives which brought about the improvements of the house and park; as it was during Jane's short time at Llwynywormwood that the spectacular stage coach was purchased and it seems that she was given control of the estate in Sir George's absences at Carmarthen and elsewhere. Anna Margaretta more than likely oversaw the extending of the house and the development of the pleasure gardens, possibly instituting the 'Lady's Walk', as she signed many of the building receipts herself. One of the later alterations to the park, following the extensive works of the previous ten or twenty years, was the building of a single arched bridge which retains the date of '1812' carved into its side. Were his wives the motivating force behind his overhauls of Llwynywormwood? Anna Margaretta died two years later in 1814 and it was commented on by later generations of the family that the estate then began a steady decline.

---

[54] NLW/MS/12357E – 'Bonedd y Cymry' by Alcwyn C. Evans Vol. 2 pp. 1385-1386 – Griffies-Williams family tree.
[55] *Cambrian Newspaper*, 28th March 1840.   [56] James, Myddfai, p. 65.   [57] Ibid. p. 69.

Sir Erasmus Griffies-Williams 1843 ~ 1870

Sir Erasmus had been born at Llwynywormwood on 22nd July 1796 and baptised at Myddfai Church on July 31st. At the age of twelve he entered Eton College where his brother John had also been educated; he then went to St John's College, Cambridge, graduating in 1818 as a Bachelor of Arts, followed by the award of a Master of Arts in 1821. [58] In 1819 Erasmus was residing at the Circus in Bath; it was here that he was married at the Abbey Church, [59] to Mrs Caroline Grubb, the widow of Lieutenant William H. Grubb, daughter of Henry Griffith and Anne Griffies of Windsor and also Erasmus's first cousin. After the ceremony the couple immediately departed for a continental tour which was predicted to last for two or three years, but which turned out to be significantly less. [60]

Caroline was described as being 'tall, and fair and extremely handsome'. [61] As a child she had been brought up in the small royal court of Queen Charlotte and her daughters at Frogmore. Princess Elizabeth had been her godmother and the other princesses had given Caroline many tokens of their affection such as a necklace, a pair of gold scissors and

Fig. 41. *Lady Caroline was described as being 'tall, and fair and extremely handsome'. This photograph was taken shortly before her death in 1866, whilst her husband was resident at St. Davids Cathedral as Chancellor Canon. Courtesy of the Noon Collection.*

---

[58] James, Myddfai, p. 202.   [59] They married on Wednesday 22nd September, *Bath Chronicle*, 23rd September 1819.
[60] *Bath Chronicle*, 23rd September 1819.   [61] Bayne & Pryme, Thackeray Family, p. 28.

six little stone hearts, each given by one of the princesses. Caroline retained these to the day she died and would fondly recall the kindnesses she had received as a young girl. It was at the age of fourteen that Caroline first met her future husband, Lieutenant Grubb, at the funeral of Princess Amelia in November 1810 where he assisted her to see the procession better. This led to a friendship, and then a love affair which caused them to elope as it was against the wishes of Caroline's father for her to marry the army officer, as he believed she was too young. When he finally relented, however, and the young couple were remarried, their happiness was not to last as the Napoleonic Wars called the young lieutenant away after a year of marriage to his death at the Battle of Waterloo. Caroline was thus a widow at the tender age of nineteen. Following her husband's death, she stayed with her recently widowed uncle, Sir George Griffies-Williams, at Llwynywormwood where both of them were united in grief. Caroline soon returned to her parents at Bath where she latterly became reacquainted with her cousin Erasmus who had also been at Llwynywormwood following the death of his mother.

Fig. 42. *The ebonised walking stick of Sir Erasmus Griffies-Williams, inscribed with a silver plaque proclaiming its owner,* 'The Hon. Sir Erasmus Williams Bart., Llwynywormwood'. *Courtesy of the Noon Collection.*

Erasmus was ordained at Salisbury on December 16th 1821 and was then appointed curate of West Dean with West Grimstead for which he was paid one hundred pounds per annum. Five years later he was nominated curate to Coombe Bissett and West Harnham. In 1829 he became fully established in the church when he was appointed Rector of Rushall. Concurrently, Erasmus was chaplain to the Dowager Lady Cawdor. Erasmus represented the family at the laying of the foundation stone of St Davids College, Lampeter on 12th August 1822, when he was with Miss Griffies-Williams, who presumably was one of his sisters.[62] The children of Erasmus and Caroline's marriage were all conceived during the 1820s. Firstly there was George Herbert who was born at Marlborough but died one year later at Bath and was removed to Marlborough with the bodies of Caroline's parents, who had previously died a few days apart from each other, for reburial. Then came Caroline Louisa and lastly the youngest child Juliana, who was born on March 1st 1825 at the Rectory, West Dean, Salisbury. It was due to Sir George's ill health that Erasmus gave his sister, Anna Margaretta away at Marlborough when she married Henry Harcourt Lyons, youngest son of William Lyons of Tenby on June 11th 1835.

On the death of his father Erasmus did not go to live at Llwynywormwood due to his ecclesiastical duties, so the house and estate were leased out. A surviving estate rent book details the various comings and goings of tenants. In 1843 there were four lodges; Fron Lodge, Penhill Lodge, Rhockllwyd Lodge and Coalbrook Lodge. In 1845 a terrible accident took place at Penhill Lodge, the Gothick east lodge to the estate. Mr and Mrs Jones were away and left three of their six daughters at home. When the eldest girl, Jane, went out to open the entrance gates for a visitor to the mansion, tragically the clothes of the younger ones caught fire and both perished in the ensuing fire. [63]

Samuel Lewis's *Topographical Dictionary of Wales* described Llwynywormwood as a handsome residence pleasantly situated on the river Ydw, and commanding some interesting prospects. [64] It was the second largest house in the parish of Myddfai, following Cilgwyn, which was situated further down the river. During the 1830s, Llwynywormwood was frequently offered to let, the Earl and Countess of Carrick leased the mansion and Lady Carrick gave birth to a son and heir there in 1834. [65] Relatives of Clive of India resided at Llwynywormwood in 1837, where a Mr George Clive's wife gave birth to a son. [66] The estate was then rented to Reverend P.H. Douglas from 1843 until November 1848 when a

[62] Journal of the Historical Society of the Church in Wales, Vol. 4, p. 107.
[63] *Carmarthen Journal*, 10th January 1845. [64] Lewis, Topographical Dictionary, p. 245.
[65] *Cambrian Newspaper*, 15th March 1834. [66] *Cambrian Newspaper*, 7th October 1837.

Mr Gordon Cecil moved in. He remained for a modicum of time as a Mrs Ellerton took up the lease in November 1849. Her daughter was married at Myddfai church to Reverend James Clancy of Claverdon, Warwickshire on 22nd April 1850. The 1851 census records that Llwynywormwood was leased to the 28-year-old Alfred Crawshay, his wife Jessy and their young son Alfred. There was also a gamekeeper, nurse and four house servants. The Crawshays were of the family of wealthy iron masters from Cyfarthfa Castle, Merthyr Tydfil.

Due to inherited mounting debts, in 1853 Sir Erasmus entered into an agreement with Mr Edward Squire, a solicitor, of 14 Great James Street, Bedford Row on behalf of the Atlas Insurance Association, to secure a mortgage amounting to £44,400 upon the greater part of Erasmus's Welsh estates. A further sum of £6,600 with interest was added in 1854 making a total debt of £51,000. Two years later an advertisement was placed in *The Welshman* during August 1855 for the tenancy of the Llwynywormwood estate; in particular the mansion house itself, which was advertised as being completely furnished and let rate, tax and tithe free. Any quantity of land could be rented and exclusive sporting rights were over four thousand acres if desired. Woodcock shooting was noted as being good and the construction of the Vale of Towy Railway from Llandovery to the South Wales Railway was underway. [67]

Sir Erasmus knew that as a pillar of society he was expected to take an interest in the locality, not only as a clergyman and landowner but also as a farmer. He was an advocate and active supporter of progressive farming techniques, encouraging local agricultural shows and various related events. He was frequently elected president of the Llandovery Agricultural Society and at their ploughing match organised in March 1841, a Chalbury plough and Biddells scarifier were brought down from Wiltshire so that the local farmers in Myddfai could test them. [68]

Caroline Louisa, Erasmus's eldest daughter was married on August 21st 1847, to William Maudley Savage, Esq. of Midsummer Norton, Somersetshire. She gave birth to a stillborn child in 1848, and then a son was born in 1851 and christened William Valentine Savage but sadly died aged only a week old. A final child was born in 1854 but was ill until its death at the age of three months, without having been named. Family members always felt that these painful events affected her outlook in later life.

Juliana, the younger daughter, married Thomas Graves-Sawle, Esq., second son of

---

[67] *The Welshman*, 23rd March 1855.
[68] James, <u>Myddfai</u>, p. 79.

Sir Joseph Sawle Graves-Sawle of Penrice, Cornwall on July 10th 1849 at Marlborough. [69]
Their seat was Steartfield, Paignton and a son was born on 28th November 1850, being
baptised Erasmus Henry Graves-Sawle after his maternal grandfather. Three further
children followed in succession; Julia Eleanor Dorothea on 19th March 1855, followed by
Marianne Rose on 29th June 1856 and Amy Trevanion born on 20th August 1859.

A huge moment of pride for both Lady Caroline and Sir Erasmus came in 1851 when a
needlepoint picture of hers inspired by Leonardo da Vinci's 'Last Supper' was shown at the
Great Exhibition at Crystal Palace. Lady Caroline was a fine needle-worker, spending most
of her spare time working on various projects, even teaching her granddaughters to sew.
Several pieces survive to this day, with many featuring the arms of the Griffies-Williams
family. These would have been displayed prominently at Llwynywormwood, such as the
fire-screen seen in figure 48. [70]

*Fig. 43. Lady Caroline Griffies-Williams's needle-point tapestry of Da Vinci's 'Last Supper', now at
St Kenwyns Church in Truro. This was given by Amy Elizabeth Noon as a gift to the church following
her death. Courtesy of St. Kenwyns Church.*

[69] The Annual Register for 1849, p. 204.
[70] See Appendix A.

Fig. 44. *Caroline Beaumont (ob. 1907), nee Griffies-Williams, eldest daughter of Sir Erasmus and Lady Caroline Griffies-Williams. Caroline was a controversial member of the family who was shunned later in life by her nieces for her interest in spiritualism. Her third marriage to Alexander Spink Beaumont, who was twenty years her junior, also compounded the situation. Alexander was a noted musician and composer, but possessed a fiery temper. For instance, during a stay at Norton House, Tenby not long after his marriage in 1873 he was charged with assault against a local man who had offended him! Courtesy of the Noon Collection.*

Fig. 45. *Juliana Graves-Sawle (1825 – 1884), nee Griffies-Williams, youngest daughter of Sir Erasmus and Lady Caroline Griffies-Williams. This miniature shows Juliana as a young woman and has been dated to the early 1840s, around the time in which her father inherited the Llwynywormwood Estate. Courtesy of the Noon Collection.*

Fig. 46. *Juliana Graves-Sawle photographed shortly before her death. It is possible that Juliana suffered from diabetes which accounts for her untimely demise at the age of fifty-nine. She was very attached to Llwynywormwood and it is her watercolour, figure 8, which is today the only accurate contemporary image to survive showing the mansion and park in their prime. Courtesy of the Noon Collection.*

Watercolours also formed part of Lady Caroline's recreations but relatively few have survived the passage of time, they depict chiefly heraldic designs and motifs. One of Sir Erasmus's private passions was a work he never fully completed; a Welsh to English lexicon. [71] A dictionary compiled by Titus Lewis in 1815 formed the reference point for his tome. Sir Erasmus had Lewis's publication delicately taken apart leaf by leaf, and then had it pasted onto blank pages so that he could expand, alter and update the contents as he

---

[71] NLW/MS/14897c.

Fig. 47. *Thomas Graves-Sawle was the second son of Sir Joseph Sawle Graves-Sawle of Penrice, Cornwall and married Juliana Griffies-Williams in 1849. The couple had four children together but their eldest, a son, died suddenly at the age of nine in 1859. Courtesy of the Noon Collection.*

wished. The laborious task must have taken many years of careful work and consideration, illustrating a great love and admiration for his native heritage and culture.

Pamphlets and letter writing were a way in which Sir Erasmus was able to extend his thoughts and opinion into the public arena. He published several that explored the role of the Church during this period; one published letter was in response to the Bishop of Exeter where he complained of the Bishop's 'acid and uncharitable' language in his

Fig. 48. *A grospoint needlework tapestry of unknown date showing the arms of the Griffies-Williams family, probably by Lady Caroline Griffies-Williams, later used as part of a fire-screen. Courtesy of the National Trust.*

Pastoral Letter. Opinions such as these were perfectly acceptable to be held privately, but this public airing of dissatisfaction led Sir Erasmus to lose some credence. His greatest desire was to receive a Bishopric but the problem was that Sir Erasmus was simply not recognised in the corridors of power and there was even confusion over his identity with another candidate by the name of Williams in one instance. [72]

Marlborough had been the principal residence of Sir Erasmus since the 1820s but in 1858 he was offered a promotion from his good friend, Bishop Thirlwall of St Davids. This was the Chancellorship, with a Canonry, of St Davids Cathedral in Pembrokeshire which

Fig. 49. *It was here at St. Davids College, Lampeter, that Sir Erasmus, and one of his young sisters, deputised for their father at the laying of the foundation stone in 1822. This engraving dates to about 1830. Author's collection.*

[72] Roger L. Brown, 'A squabbling Squarson and a contentious Chancellor', <u>The Journal of the Pembrokeshire Historical Society</u>, VIII (1998 - 1999), p. 34.

Fig. 50. *Rev. Sir Erasmus Griffies-Williams (1796 – 1870), 2ⁿᵈ Baronet of Llwynywormwood, painted in 1858 by E.U. Eddis as a gift for Lady Caroline Griffies-Williams, following subscription from the inhabitants of Marlborough. Courtesy of the National Trust.*

was offered and readily accepted despite Erasmus's advancing years. This position was distinct from the Chancellorship of the Diocese, which was a legal post, and was linked, with the role of a divinity lecturer to the clergy of the Diocese. [73] Sir Erasmus took up residence on 16th May and henceforth endeavoured 'to cleanse this worse than Augean Stable'. [74] It has been suggested that Bishop Thirlwall had appointed Sir Erasmus to undertake this role of reformer and corrector, especially noting that the Dean, Dr Llewellyn Lewellin, was there only during vacations from St Davids College, Lampeter. Erasmus's track record had shown him to be a promoter of hard work with great drive, something which was needed at the rather sleepy and neglected Cathedral of St Davids during the Dean's long absences.

It was then that the inhabitants of Marlborough presented to Lady Caroline a portrait of her husband by E.U. Eddis, which now hangs in the National Trust Office at Llandeilo (See figure 50). Sir Erasmus had it engraved and copies were distributed to several members of the family as well as the press. Being much closer to Llwynywormwood, Sir Erasmus became a much more frequent visitor and took delight in being able to enjoy his boyhood home once more. Juliana's only son, Erasmus Henry, died at the age of eight on 15th January 1859, a bitter blow to Sir Erasmus and Lady Caroline. Bishop Thirlwall wrote that despite suffering *'a very severe blow in the loss of a grandson, who was the joy and hope of his life... Sir Erasmus's ...charity and attention to the poor of St Davids'* was immense and it helped him to cope with the sorrow he felt. [75]

Erasmus must have arrived like St Patrick in pagan Ireland; his views and proposals did not necessarily reflect those of the indigenous population. His letters to the Ecclesiastical Commissioners detail what he considered to be the chief troubles with the Cathedral; namely the officials and that St Davids was the Welsh St Helena. He wrote they 'were so inbedded in inherited neglect as to be astonished at being required to do their duty...the Cathedral is left in the hands of a child not 3 feet high. The Clerk seldom attends, and when he does, he leaves the Cathedral during the service. The Verger complains *'it is very hard that he should attend every time (i.e. 152 times out of 730) for when he was appointed the Canons seldom attended'!!! The dogwhipper is disabled from age and infirmity from attending. I say no more at present. I have at last succeeded in getting a Chapter in the beginning of next month for the purpose of seeking some reform of these*

[73] Brown, *'A squabbling Squarson'*, p. 35.
[74] Ibid. p. 35.
[75] Bayne & Pryme, Thackeray family, p. 34.

and other more serious matters, and if I fail I must seek the Visitorial aid of my excellent Bishop.' [76]

The great architect, Sir George Gilbert Scott also came under fire when he was approached regarding works at the Cathedral; Erasmus did not agree that a two to three hour examination of the tower could be adequate. Thus the detailed estimate of £4,800 for the repairs was queried. A remarkable account of Sir Erasmus is left by Mrs Nares, the daughter of his adversary Dean Llewellyn Lewellin. She says that Erasmus *'had an exaggerated idea of his own importance as a Baronet, and tried to supersede the Dean on many occasions, which became rather inconvenient; so Dr L. had to make him understand, that whatever he might be outside, inside the Cathedral he (Dr L.) was supreme! But directly his back was turned and the coast clear, we heard the most amusing stories of how Sir Erasmus tried to keep the Cathedral officials in order, even going as far as to lock the organ loft when the organist had offended him, and the services had to be conducted without music! But his standing grievance was against the Ecclesiastical Commissioners, and he would inveigh by the hour against their delinquencies to anyone who would listen to him!'* [77] Sir Erasmus's dislike of the Dean however can be epitomised in a verse given as an epitaph written in one of his letters:

Whether he lives or whether he dies
Nobody laughs and nobody cries
Where he is gone and how he fares
Nobody knows and nobody cares. [78]

Fig. 51. *Sir Erasmus was very impressed by and proud of the generous gift of his portrait. To commemorate the event he commissioned a limited number of engravings to be made for distribution to family and friends. This particular copy was presented to St. Davids Cathedral and was personally signed by Erasmus. Notice how Erasmus has his right hand placed on the Welsh Bible. Courtesy of St. Davids Cathedral.*

[76] NLW/SD/Ch/let/471-2.
[77] E. N. Nares, Pleasant Memories of Eminent Churchmen, (Carmarthen, 1890), p. 42.
[78] NLW/SD/Ch/let/431.

So much angst was caused by the Dean suddenly descending on the Cathedral during those spasmodic periods in which he was in residence. He took control of the proceedings whenever he was there without consulting Erasmus properly, further widening the gulf between them. Erasmus goes onto say that it was '...only Temper that urges them to show their importance over the clergy who presume to think for themselves. They are abominable Tyrants and Bullies but they shall not bully me with Impunity.' [79]

Even the large Chancellor's House in St Davids caused problems. It had been built by a Canon Melville at his own cost in 1846 and Erasmus felt that it was a house befitting a gentleman with an income of £3000 per year rather than a cleric on £350. The Commissioners claimed ownership of the house as part of the capitular property. This Erasmus felt, was rather frivolous and retained only to justify future seizure of property. Until their claim was either established or abandoned, Erasmus refused to repair or insure the property. *'The roof leaked so that most of the bedrooms were damp...substantial fires in every room could not obviate the volumes of cold rushing in...the water dripping from the ceiling of the dining room and landing had to be collected in buckets...while the library had to remain unfurnished and unoccupied for a similar reason...shoes left there for even a few days would be found covered in damp.'* [80] He wrote to the Commissioners in a moment of despair to *'take the house, if you can...and let me go from a place where labour and sorrow are my portion and only my gratification is my calling.'* [81]

Meanwhile, at Llwynywormwood a new tenant had appeared in the form of Reverend Edward Nugent Bree, described, according to the census returns of 1861, as a 'clergyman without care of souls'. Bree had been born on 14th January 1807 in Stebbing, Essex. Due to ill health he had retired from his parish of All Saints, Hereford to Llwynywormwood in 1859; he lived in the mansion with his wife Elizabeth and children, Annie, Miles and Alice. Harriet Lampden was the governess, Ann Williams the cook and Mary Jones the dairymaid. Under the rule of Reverend Bree, several farmers on the estate were removed from their holdings for no reason except that Bree wanted to consolidate a dozen farms into one. A tenant was interviewed some thirty-five years later during the Royal Commission on lands in Wales; he stated that *'Mr Bree, Clerk in Holy Orders came to live at Llwynywormwood... He rented the twelve adjoining farms...for the term of twenty one years, at a higher rent than was paid by the tenants. All the tenants in several cottages were compelled to leave,*

---

[79] Brown, '*A squabbling Squarson*', p. 45.
[80] Ibid. p. 42.
[81] Ibid. p. 42.

but before the end of the seven years he became insolvent, and absconded without paying his rent, and left the buildings in a very bad state.' [82] Bree had spent most of his money on pulling down fences and walls in a misguided attempt at agricultural improvement, which may have resulted in his filing for bankruptcy.

It was said that due to Reverend Bree's harmful activities, a large part of the Myddfai parish became depopulated. Bree fled to New Zealand, where his brother was residing, breaking his twenty-one year contract with Sir Erasmus after only six years and nine months. [83] Erasmus had given Bree the choice of releasing himself from the contract after the first seven years, rent to be paid every quarter but Bree absconded three months before his contract ended and robbed Erasmus of a quarter's rent. Even by 1894 only six of the twelve affected tenements had been occupied, while the others remained in ruins. There were extensive areas of land where the soil was neglected which, if had been properly cultivated would have produced treble the results, and would have been sufficient to maintain many families. [84]

Not long after the death of her grandson, Lady Caroline visited Bishop Thirlwall at the Bishop's Palace, Abergwili, with her husband's cousin who described her on this particular occasion; *'she was a handsome, stately woman, some way past middle age, a great needleworker, very gentle and affectionate. Bishop Thirlwall had a great regard for her...'* [85] Caroline died on December 31st 1866 and her good friend Bishop Thirlwall sent a heartfelt letter of condolence to Sir Erasmus.

Fig. 52. *A lock of Lady Caroline's hair, cut by her grieving daughter Juliana on her deathbed, is still preserved by descendants of the family. The rich auburn hair contains surprisingly little grey for a woman over the age of seventy. Her mother, Anne Griffies, similarly did not turn grey even into old age. Courtesy of the Noon Collection.*

[82] Royal Commission on Lands in Wales and Monmouthshire. <u>Minutes of evidence taken before the Royal Commission on Lands in Wales and Monmouthshire – Vol. III</u>, (1895, London), p.149.
[83] Ibid., p. 174.   [84] Ibid., p.149.   [85] Bayne & Pryme, <u>Thackeray family</u>, p. 29.

Fig. 53. *Another needlework depicting the Griffies-Williams Coat of Arms which originally came from Llwynywormwood and was bequeathed to the National Trust under the terms of Amy Elizabeth Noon's will. Courtesy of the National Trust.*

As for Sir Erasmus, his brother Herbert, then living at Llwynhelig near Llandeilo, recalled that '*he was a man of great energy, and during the twelve years he resided at St Davids he devoted himself zealously to the restoration of the Cathedral which had fallen into a very dilapidated state. Alas! However, he was not spared to see its completion…* ' [86] Another relative remembered him as a 'tall and handsome man, with dignified yet easy manners, of good natural abilities, well read, and possessed of great conversational powers. He was tenderly attached to his fair, gentle wife; and after her death felt so keenly the loneliness of his isolated home – nearly three hundred miles from London… that he took a house at Tenby for occasional residence.' [87] This house was then used by Sir Erasmus's eldest daughter Caroline who had been widowed in 1867.

Llanfihangel ym Myddfai was the traditional place of worship and burial site for the family (see figure 54). In 1866 Sir Erasmus proposed to build a whole new north transept to the Church with a family vault beneath it. A parish meeting was convened, approving the plan and permission was given by the Bishop with detailed architectural drawings finalised. [88] However, nothing came to fruition, possibly due to the death of Lady Caroline or lack of funding for a project, which would have cemented the status of the Griffies-Williams family in Myddfai.

A tantalising glimpse of Sir Erasmus's eldest daughter Caroline comes from a letter written by Mrs Harries of Aberglasney near Llandeilo during March 1870. She states that during the Carmarthen Hunt Week, she had had Mrs Caroline Savage staying with her at Aberglasney, and with regard to her hunting she goes on to say that '… she is as odd as her father & I think that is saying a great deal …' [89] This relates to the fact that Sir Erasmus was very much against hunting and this was looked disapprovingly upon by his neighbours, and it seems that his eldest daughter shared the same sentiment.

On the night of 30th November 1870, Sir Erasmus was staying at the Castle Hotel, Llandovery when he suddenly died of an apoplectic fit, at the age of seventy-six. A letter from R. Augustus of Court Cottage, Llandovery details the visit of Major Watkins of Breconshire who came on 5th December 1870, '*…he was very low in consequence of the death of Sir Erasmus Williams Bart who died at the Castle in this town on the 30th Nov and is to be buried at Mothvey tomorrow. Lady Williams who died some years ago and was buried in Pembrokeshire is to be disinterred and brought up to Mothvey to be placed by the side of her husband tomorrow…*' [90]

---

[86] Ibid., p. 33.   [87] Ibid. p. 34.   [88] NLW/CWR/SD/F/550.
[89] NLW/DolaucothiCorrespondence3/L3710.   [90] NLW/Glansevin/2221.

Fig. 54. *Sir Erasmus was buried on 6th December 1870 at Mydffai Parish Church. His wife, Lady Caroline, had died four years earlier and her body was disinterred from its resting place in St. Davids and was brought back to Myddfai for burial. Both husband and wife were interred together at a joint burial service. Author's collection.*

So ended the life of Sir Erasmus. Herbert Vaughan in the 1920s wrote a disparaging description of Sir Erasmus, he stated that Erasmus was *'was pompous, litigious, and by no means a general favourite.'* [91] Vaughan wrongly looks back at one of the last Squarsons [92] with a sad note of ridicule; mocking Sir Erasmus as a pompous, litigious and arrogant man whose quarrelsome nature was his downfall. However, this is not the case. Sir Erasmus was a man under enormous pressure, who stoically tried to salvage the dignity of his family following estate mismanagement by his brother and to a lesser degree his father.

Even after succeeding to the Baronetcy and the estates in 1843, he had no alternative but to remain in Marlborough to support his family with a steady income, which he could not have done from Llwynywormwood, on its own revenue alone, following the debts left behind by his brother and father. Sir Erasmus was also responsible for the annuities of his siblings, which must have created a financial burden; in the end he was forced to heavily mortgage the estates. Nonetheless, Erasmus was an assiduous man who was forward thinking and acutely aware of his duties and position. He was, most unusually, fluent in both written and spoken Welsh, as illustrated by his uncompleted but far advanced lexicon. Those who knew him well and were employed by him thought very highly of this particular Squarson and his ways.

Reading the letters of Sir Erasmus, one detects a sense of sadness and bitterness towards the way his life had turned out. He did not succeed in becoming a Bishop and had to settle for a lesser position in a remote Cathedral. This seems to have been an annoyance as even in the year of his death, he was hoping to be appointed Bishop of St Asaph. [93] His time at St Davids was thwarted with arguments and petty behaviour on all sides. A letter written in 1864 perhaps displays this sorrow he so deeply felt… *'I think I shall take the wings of a dove and fly away and be then at rest. It is only death and desolation here. It is bad at my old age to meet with the treatment I do, but I can bear and forbear…'* [94]

---

[91] See Appendix B for full transcript.   [92] A Squarson is an amalgamation of the words 'squire' and 'parson'; it denotes a certain class of gentry or landowners who also held a clerical office.
[93] Brown, *'A squabbling Squarson'*, pp. 34 – 35.   [94] NLW/SD/Ch/let/486.

The Heirs of Llwynywormwood 1870 - 1913

General Watkin Lewis Griffies-Williams, the fourth son of Sir George, succeeded to be the third baronet on the death of his brother. He had entered the Indian Army as Ensign, rising to the rank of Lieutenant in 1819 at the age of sixteen, serving latterly with the Third Light Infantry of the Madras Establishment throughout the Burmese Wars in 1824-26. Watkin was present at the storming of Rangoon and the Syrian Pagodas and commanded his regiment in person at the attack on the stockade at Seet-Town in 1826, for which he received a medal and was thanked in Orders. Some years afterwards, in 1844, Watkin served at the siege and storming of Punnullah and at the capture of Munnohor. He also served in the second Burmese War as Brigadier in 1852 and at the close commanded the troops on the frontier beyond Tongu for which he also received a medal. [95] At the time of his inheriting the baronetcy, Watkin was living at 38, Elgin Road, Kensington Park Gardens where he had retired from the army many years earlier. The death of his only surviving brother, Reverend David Herbert Thackeray Griffies-Williams, [96] on April 8th 1877 was an appalling blow as he would have succeeded Watkin. Thus, the baronetcy became extinct, as not one of Sir George's five sons left a surviving male heir.

Fig. 55. *Thomas Graves-Sawle survived his wife for some twenty-seven years. This photograph was taken in 1903 when he was aged seventy-seven. Thomas Graves-Sawle died on 2nd February 1911 and was buried at St Austell in Cornwall. Courtesy of the Noon Collection.*

[95] Letter from General Sir Watkin Lewis Griffies-Williams, 9th December 1870 to Debretts Peerage.
[96] Always known as Herbert.

Fig. 56. *Julia Eleanor Graves-Sawle (1855 – 1927), eldest daughter of Juliana and Thomas Graves-Sawle, as a young girl, circa 1860. It forms a pair with figure 57. Courtesy of the Noon Collection.*

Fig. 57. *Marianne Graves-Sawle (1856 – 1941), second daughter of Juliana and Thomas Graves-Sawle, as a child. Marianne never married but continued to remain close to her siblings and her only niece, Amy Elizabeth Noon. Courtesy of the Noon Collection.*

The last Will and Testament of Sir Erasmus had been made on the eleventh of November 1869. All of his estates were bequeathed in trust to two trustees; Frederick Browne and George Henry Williams, both solicitors from London. Firstly, they were directed to pay by half yearly payments to his daughter Caroline the sum of twelve hundred pounds per year. She was also granted the full use and enjoyment of Norton House, Tenby, together with the garden that had recently been purchased by Erasmus. [97] Six hundred pounds was set aside for the improvement and enlargement of Norton House if the need arose. All of this

---

[97] Norton House was already Caroline's home following her widowhood.

was rent-free so long as Caroline continued in occupation or decided alternatively to take up residence at Llwynywormwood, which was specified as being the house, gardens, pleasure grounds, woods and lands, which formed the estate, and would cost £200 per annum. All furniture from each specific house was to remain with the respective properties. If Caroline chose Llwynywormwood, then Norton House would pass to Juliana.

Juliana was directed to be given eight hundred pounds per annum plus Norton House or Llwynywormwood according to the desire of Caroline, a year following the death of Sir Erasmus. Thomas Graves-Sawle was bequeathed fifty pounds as a mark of affection and was assigned all shooting and sporting rights over all the estates but this excluded hunting, which Sir Erasmus strongly objected to. Juliana and Thomas' daughters were awarded an annuity of forty pounds and on the death of one the money would go into the general or 'hotchpot' fund.

An annuity of fifty pounds was to be paid to Sir Erasmus's brother, Reverend Herbert Griffies-Williams of Llwynhelig for the use of their sister Eliza Maria Decima, the wife of William Holwell Short, as Sir Erasmus expressly stated that his brother would be a kind sibling and not allow any interference with his sister by her

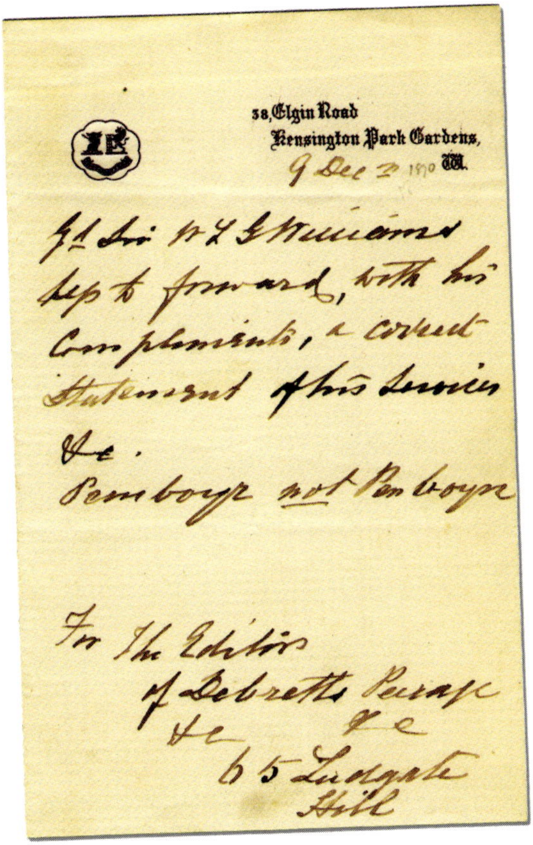
58, Elgin Road
Kensington Park Gardens,
W.
9 Dec 1870

Gl Sir W L G Williams begs to forward, with his Compliments, a correct Statement of his Services &c.
Pemboyre not Penboyre

For the Editor
of Debretts Peerage
&c &c
65 Ludgate
Hill

Fig. 58. *General Sir Watkin Lewis Griffies-Williams's letter dated 9th December 1870 to Debretts Peerage correcting them on his volume entry. Author's collection.*

husband or anyone else. [98] Reverend Herbert was left £300 himself, the interest of which would be his for his lifetime and then after his death divided between his three daughters. Another £300 was left to Mary Anne Caroline Griffies Vaughan which after her death would be divided between her three daughters, Caroline, Florence and Amy. £100 was left to Mrs Lyons, another sister and after her death to her daughter Agnes. Edmund Kent, Sir Erasmus's nephew, was bequeathed £100 in memory of his late mother, Anne Griffies-Williams.

Caroline and Juliana were both appointed executors of the will and were given one year to see to the payment of the legacies. Minor estates in the counties of Wiltshire, Cardigan and the city of St Davids were available to be sold by the trustees for the discharge of every legal obligation and for an accumulating fund. This was together with the thinning of woodland and plantations, plus any windfalls and the residue of any property not required for the payment of claimants, so that all real estate would be ultimately free from

Fig. 59. Amy Trevanion Graves-Sawle as a young woman, during the 1870s. Amy was attractive and it is said that she inherited her looks from her grandmother, Lady Caroline Griffies-Williams. Courtesy of the Noon Collection.

Fig. 60. Amy Trevanion Graves-Sawle (1859 – 1938), youngest child of Juliana and Thomas Graves-Sawle as a young girl. Amy was the closest of all to her parents, in particular her mother. This photograph shows her standing with her paternal grandmother, Lady Graves-Sawle. Courtesy of the Noon Collection.

---

[98] Sir George's fourth daughter, Eliza Maria Decima married William Holwell Short Esq., eldest son of the Reverend Lawrence Short, of Ashover Rectory, Derbyshire on 26th March 1831 at the church of St Mary, Islington. Eliza Maria was one of the favourite daughters of Sir George and also a beloved sister of Erasmus. From *The Times*, April 9th, 1831.

all debt. However, it was strictly forbidden for any trees to be cut down on the Llwynywormwood demesne or park on any account.

It was the greatest objective for Sir Erasmus that the family of Llwynywormwood would be re-established and given the proper station in the county. He stipulated that all who took on the estate *'would take the name of Erasmus Williams and wear the arms of Llwynywormwood, trusting that whoever should come into possession would possess the same feelings and the same desire to uphold the family'*, [99] in the way Sir Erasmus had done. It was the freeing of the estate from all demands and debts, which was the greatest concern for Sir Erasmus. It does seem apparent from the will that he did not expect to die so suddenly and so soon after it had been drawn up. No provision had been made for the leasing of the estate to raise money to pay all of the bequests. Also at the time of his death, Sir Erasmus was under contract for the sale and purchase of certain real estates. Clearly Erasmus had been under great financial strain and had struggled to keep the estate buoyant.

The picture of tapestry depicting 'The Last Supper' by Leonardo da Vinci, which was the workmanship of Lady Caroline, and had been exhibited at the Great Exhibition of 1851 was to be preserved in perpetuity at Llwynywormwood (see figure 43). This was to be an heirloom for the family, indicative of the skill and patience employed in such a laborious work of art. Sir Erasmus's portrait by Eddis was also to be preserved at the mansion house together with a gold snuff box given by the inhabitants of several towns in Wiltshire as a memorial for the services rendered to the subscribers of the portrait in his capacity as a member of the Odd Fellows Friendly Society. A Welsh bible and prayer book given by the children of the Marlborough National Schools was to be an heirloom too.

By 13th February 1871, the trustees, Frederick Browne and George Henry Williams had filed a bill of complaint against the executors Caroline and Juliana. [100] Questions had been raised over the execution of the trusts and the administration of the estate and the trustees felt unable safely to act out the execution of the trusts except by the direction of the Court of Chancery. A sale of land followed later in 1871 after the decision of the Browne v. Savage case to raise funds for the payment of the legacies. In 1853 and 1854 a large mortgage had been raised and, in 1873, this had been transferred to the trustees on the occasion of a new mortgage.

Sir Erasmus's untimely death had left the estate in turmoil, making it difficult for

---

[99] From the will of Sir Erasmus.
[100] NLW/Cwmgwili/1526.

Fig. 61. *Following her engagement in 1891 to William Prinn Noon, Amy Trevanion and her fiancé posed for portrait photographs to celebrate the occasion. This image is a companion for figure 63. Courtesy of the Noon Collection.*

Fig. 62. *Julia Eleanor Graves-Sawle married Francis Rashleigh Rodd of Trebartha Hall in 1882. They had no children so lavished much attention on their niece, Amy Elizabeth Noon. Courtesy of the Noon Collection.*

Caroline and Juliana to administer the directions set down by their father's will. The trustees requested that the Court would direct and administer the trusts, real and personal estate and also appoint a receiver to gather in the rents and profits of the estate together with garnering the personal estate. It was ordered by the Court that accounts and enquiries be made into the personal estate not bequeathed to Caroline and Juliana. An account of Sir Erasmus's debts and funeral expenses, and an enquiry as to what parts of the real estate and personal estate which were outstanding, were made available. Interestingly, it was investigated whether it would be proper with regards to the Will for

Fig. 63. *William Prinn Noon had received his first army commission on February 11ᵗʰ 1870, being promoted to lieutenant a year later and by 1897 had advanced to the rank of lieutenant-colonel. He saw active service in 1879 with the transport staff during the Afghan war and was present at the occupation of Candahar as well as at Ahmed Kheyl. Courtesy of the Noon Collection.*

part of the real estate to be sold and what part of the rents and profits could be accumulated for the discharge of legal obligations. It had to be established who was actually the heir at law at the time of death and who the heir was subsequently. The trustees questioned whether the grandchildren of Sir Erasmus were living at the date of the will.

It was not until August 1872 that the questions were answered and the annuities were in arrears to the amount of £2706 15s 0d. By this time, George Henry Williams had died and Caroline had married Captain Alexander Spink Beaumont. Alexander had been born in 1843 in Manchester, the son of General Beaumont of the 92ⁿᵈ Highlanders, and served with the Royal Welsh Fusiliers. They had met whilst he was lodging at Norton House and unusual circumstances brought them together. Caroline, due to her traumatic losses, had converted to spiritualism and with her new husband proceeded to publish accounts of their psychical experiences in leading journals and publications. This led to a division within the family, since her father had been a leading churchman and her mother a devout Christian.

Alexander wrote that *'about September 1873, when my father was living at 57 Inverness Terrace, I was sitting one evening about eight thirty pm in the large dining room. At the table, facing me, with their backs to the door, were seated my mother, sister and a friend Mrs W. Suddenly I seemed to see my wife bustling in through the door of the back sitting room, which was in view from my position. She was in a mauve dress. I got up to meet her, though much astonished, as I believed her to be at Tenby. As I rose, my mother said: "Who is that?", not (I think) seeing anyone herself, but seeing that I did. I exclaimed: "Why, it is Carrie!" and advanced to meet her. As I advanced the figure disappeared. On enquiry I found that my wife was spending that evening at a friend's house, in a mauve dress which I had most certainly never seen. I had never seen her dressed in that colour. My wife recollected that at that time she was talking with some friends about me, much regretting my absence, as there was going to be dancing and I had promised to play for them. I had been unexpectedly detained in London.'*

A friend, Florence Whipham, had been present at the dinner and testified by letter that *'as far as I can recollect, Captain Beaumont was sitting talking when he looked up and gave a start. His mother asked him what was the matter. He replied, "I saw my wife walk across the end of the room but that is nothing; she often appears to people, her servants have seen her several times." The room we were in was a double dining room, one end was lit with gas and the other where Mrs Beaumont appeared was comparatively dark. No-one else saw her except her husband. Mrs Beaumont was at the time in Wales and this happened in Inverness Terrace, Bayswater.'* Validating this, Caroline recalled that the incident in question: *'I distinctly remember hearing from my husband, either the next day or the second day after his experience; and in his letter he asked, "what were you doing at such an hour on such a night?" I was able to recall that I was standing in a group of friends and we were regretting his absence. I was in a mauve dress, which I am confident that he could never have seen.'*

Fig. 64. *This photograph shows Amy Trevanion Noon nursing her newborn daughter, Amy Elizabeth Noon (1893 – 1979). It was taken on 13th September 1893 in Muree, India, where William Prinn Noon was serving with the army. Courtesy of the Noon Collection.*

Fig. 65. *Here is Amy Elizabeth Noon, 'Elly', with her three pet dogs around the time in which her parents retired to Plymouth. This photograph was slotted into one of the pages of Amy's well-thumbed bible, given on the occasion of her confirmation, by her godmothers Marianne Graves-Sawle and Elizabeth Shilson. It is dated 21st November 1909. Courtesy of the Noon Collection.*

Captain Beaumont added that he had never had any other hallucinations or psychic experience except on the occasion next described. *'In 1871 I was staying at Norton House Tenby for the first time and had just gone to bed and was wide awake. I had the candle on my right side and was reading. At the foot of the bed and to the right was a door, which was locked and as I learnt afterwards pasted up on the other side through this I saw the figure of my future wife (the lady of the house) enter, draped in white from head to foot. Oddly enough I was not specially startled my idea was that someone was ill and that she had to come and get something out of the room. I averted my head and when I looked up again the apparition was gone. I suppose that I saw it for two or three seconds.'*

Caroline went on to explain that *'In 1872, two or three months after my marriage, Captain Beaumont and I returned from London to Tenby. I went up into my dressing room and gave the keys of my luggage to my servant, Ellen Bassett. I was standing before the looking glass with my back turned to her and I heard her utter a little sharp cry. I turned round saying "what's the matter?" and saw her with my nightcap in her hand. She said "Oh, nothing nothing" and I went downstairs. The day after my husband saw her taking off the paper which pasted up the door between my bedroom and the dressing room. He said, "what are you doing?" She said she was opening that door. He said "Why, the first night that I slept in this house I saw your mistress walk through that door." (I must explain that Captain Beaumont had been a guest in this house on a good many occasion before our marriage. On the occasion mentioned he had imagined that perhaps someone was ill in the house, and that I had entered his room to get something thinking him sure to be asleep.) Then the maid told him that she had seen me the night before we came home – she did not know exactly what day we were coming and had been sleeping in the same bed as he had been in when he saw me. She was going to step into bed when she saw me enter through the door with a nightcap on and a candle in my hand. She was so terrified that she rushed out of the room by the other door and told the other servants she was sure I was dead. They comforted her as well as they could but she would not return to the room. The cause of her crying out, when I heard her do so was that in unpacking, she recognised the identical nightcap the apparition had worn. The curious point is that the nightcap was one that I had bought in London and had not mentioned to her and was perfectly unlike any that I had ever worn before. It had three frills. I had been accustomed to wear nightcaps of coloured muslin without frills. The same servant some months after the nightcap incident went into the kitchen and said to the other servants "We shall have news of missus today; I've just seen her standing in the dining room door, she had on a black velvet bonnet and black cloak." (We had been in London some weeks.) This occurred about nine o'clock a.m. About ten thirty she received a telegram from us to saw we should be at home that evening; the telegram was sent from Paddington station as we waited for our train. The bonnet and cloak had been bought in town without her knowledge. The maid was with me for years and certainly not nervous or hysterical. I have now parted with her for some years.'*

On the 16th November 1872 an order was made allowing the Judge to decide what parts of the real estate should be sold and that any of the parties were at liberty to apply in Chambers for the appointment of a new trustee to replace George Henry Williams. By June 1876, Frederick Browne wanted to retire from his role as trustee and authorised the sale of Norton House in Tenby to Caroline. A year later, Amelius Arthur Hopkinson and Charles Shilson were appointed trustees. In 1879 a hearing was convened, calling for the sale and of sufficient land to raise funds for the estate and annuities. [101] It seemed that due to the mortgages, the estate was not able to afford to pay the annuities and its own running costs. The sale took place on Saturday 23rd August at the Ivy Bush in Carmarthen town; one thousand four hundred and ninety three acres were put up for sale in twenty-four lots, the estimated income was thought to be £1,130 per year. A reduction in the outgoings came on 18th February 1880 when Sir Erasmus's sister, Eliza Maria Decima, who was towards the end of her life certified insane, passed away.

During early February 1882, Julia Eleanor Dorothea married Francis Rashleigh Rodd. It was covenanted to 'bar the entail' of Julia in relation to the event of her having a son and heir who would inherit all of the estate. On 16th August took place the final of three sales of the outlying portions of the Llwynywormwood estate, comprising 2,850 acres. It included sixty freehold houses, shops and cottages including the Llandovery public houses of the Three Horse Shoes, Grey House and White Lion. [102]

Juliana remembered as a child the old family pedigree in Welsh which was kept at Llwynywormwood and that 'it was long enough to reach from one side of the dining room, across the hall, and drawing room. It was one of the old Welsh pedigrees, more curious

---

[101] NLW/Cwmgwili/1515.
[102] CRO/JohnFrancis/SC/761.

Fig. 66. *Amy Elizabeth Noon at the age of twenty-one. This photograph was taken at Trebartha Hall during September 1914, shortly after the breakout of World War One. Courtesy of the Noon Collection.*

than useful.' [103] Juliana died on 9th February 1884 at the age of fifty-eight at Southernhay, Devon, leaving £13,687 and the Will was proved by her husband Thomas Graves-Sawle, although the probate was granted under certain conditions.

At Llwynywormwood in 1871, only the gamekeeper and his family were in the mansion house. It is not clear whether they were employed by the trustees of the estate to look after the mansion or if they were tenants. By 1881, Thomas Lloyd Morgan and his niece, Mary Livia Howells were the tenants and employed two servants. Morgan was still the principal tenant in 1891, living with two servants. During March 1898, Thomas Lloyd

---

[103] Bayne & Pryme, Thackeray family, p. 31.

Morgan was declared bankrupt [104] and during August the contents of Llwynywormwood were put up for sale. The trustees of Sir Erasmus's will sanctioned the sale of the contents by public auction on Tuesday 30th August 1898 at the mansion house itself, in pursuance of an Order of the High Court of Chancery made pursuant to the suit of Browne v. Savage on 23rd July. Everything was to be sold including fine Chippendale, mahogany, carved rosewood, old oak and much rare furniture. Pictures, antique china and glass were on view in the Hall, Library, Dining Room, Drawing Room, Servants Hall, Butler's Pantry and seven bedrooms. Unfortunately, no further details or even a copy of the catalogue have come to light regarding this sale. [105]

By 1901 the main house was lived in by a tenant farmer, John Thomas and his family of five. An advertisement was placed in *The Welshman* newspaper regarding the sale of standing timber, comprising 'very fine oak, larch, beech, Scotch elm, sycamore and chestnut timbers…growing on Llwynywormwood…all the above timber is easily accessible to main roads, and the Woodman, Tom Hughes, Mothvey, will show the same and the roads over which the timber must be carried away…' [106] The auction took place at the North Western Hotel, Llandovery, at 2.30pm on November 9th 1906.

At this time, the recently widowed Leticia Davies moved into Llwynywormwood Mansion to act as housekeeper. She took with her her three children; Thomas, Isaac and Joseph. Isaac remembered that there was a marble statue of a lady 'lighting the way' on the main staircase, something which local people remembered right up to the 1940s. Isaac would walk to school every day from Llwynywormwood to Llandovery, taking with him, on his first day at school, the young Davey Thomas Lewis, a future owner of Llwynywormwood, and later they became good friends. In the 1950s, Isaac would visit the home farm with his own children, where bacon sides were hanging in the kitchen and the orchard was always fruitful. [107]

Caroline died on 13th April 1907 at South Norwood Park, south-east London, and it was then that the three granddaughters of Sir Erasmus began to decide what to do with the estate. The residue of the Llwynywormwood estate was put up for sale on 16th July 1909.[108] Two thousand acres including the mansion house itself were offered and it was estimated that the annual income was in the region of £200. A pitifully small amount reflective of the very severe depression in farming at this time.

---

[104] *The Welshman*, 5th April 1898.   [105] *The Welshman*, 12th August 1898.
[106] *The Western Mail*, 5th November 1906.   [107] H/MS/L/51206.   [108] *Carmarthen Journal*, July 2nd 1909.

Fig. 67. *Amy Elizabeth at Trebartha Hall, Launceston, Cornwall during the early 1920s. Miss Noon is the statuesque lady standing second from the left, next to her aunt, Julia Eleanor Rodd. This photograph was given by Douglas Mann, husband of Ellie Noon's goddaughter, the late Evelyn May Stanhope Mann. Authors Collection.*

The sale catalogue stated that Llwynywormwood *'stands in a well-sheltered position, overlooking the whole of the beautiful Llwynywormwood Park and is approached by a carriage drive with three entrances. On the ground floor…there is an Entrance Hall, Library, Drawing Room and Conservatory. On the first floor – eight bedrooms, nursery, bathroom and two W.C's. Above are five bedrooms and lumber room. The domestic offices comprise – Servant's hall, Butler's Pantry, Kitchen, Larder, Scullery, Dairy, Laundry and outer Kitchen…The Stabling Premises comprise – five stalls and two loose boxes, Saddle and Harness Room, Coach House and Men's Room over. The kitchen gardens and lands adjoin the house, and comprise six and a half acres…The homestead and farm buildings consist of a stone build and slated dwelling house with Kitchen,*

Fig. 68. *Julia Eleanor Rodd's grave in 1927, from a photograph taken by Elly Noon. Her five years of widowhood were spent with her sister Amy and niece Elly in Plymouth, where she passed away in 1927. The funeral took place at North Hill, Cornwall where the little church was packed with mourners who paid tribute to the memory of one who had been a great benefactor to the district. Courtesy of the Noon Collection.*

Back-Kitchen, Parlour, Dairy and Four Bedrooms. A very large and lofty barn. An extremely roomy and very large Beast-house and Calf-Shed, Piggeries. A new corrugated iron stock shed, Granary, Implement Shed &c. The Farm, Park and Land are now in the occupation of Mr William Lewis, at the yearly rental of £108 10s. 0d...

The Mansion House is in hand and has been for some years unoccupied, except by a caretaker. There are three lodges known as Entrance Lodge, in the occupation of Mr Thomas Jones, and the Round Lodge, in the occupation of Mr Thomas Bruce, each at the yearly rental of £4 including rates; and Penhill Lodge, which is in hand...' [109]

The house as so often in those difficult economic times did not sell, but much land did; Thomas Williams Rogers paid eight thousand pounds for much of the park on 29th September 1909. Solicitors acting for the purchasers noted that the will of Sir Erasmus seemed to be carelessly abstracted and it was thought 'to be clerical errors for they are an absurdity as they stand.' [110] The family solicitors, Shilson Coode and Co., responded that the will was correctly abstracted and that there were no clerical errors. It had been prepared by Sir Erasmus himself but it was not 'very correctly expressed', however it was made clear that the estates were to pass to the eldest daughter of the youngest daughter and her heirs male. [111] Llwynywormwood house, farm, some land and three lodges remained with the trustees until January 1st 1913, when they were purchased by Rogers, who had previously acquired the park and surrounding land.

After the family had sold the estate they continued with their lives as before. Juliana's husband, Thomas Graves-Sawle died on 2nd February 1911, aged eighty-five, and was buried at St Austell. The family were particularly proud of his fine coffin which contained an inner casket of cedar lined with satin, whilst the outer coffin was of unpolished oak with heavy brass mountings. Caroline's husband, Captain Alexander Spink Beaumont died on 4th September 1913 at Crossland, Beckenham, Kent at the age of seventy. Alex, as he was known, was a noted amateur violinist and composer; his London home with Caroline was renowned for its musical recitals and artistic evenings. After serving in India, Alexander retired and travelled extensively with his wife. He published many pieces for violin and piano under the pseudonym Charles Woolhouse, mostly to good reviews. Alex and Caroline, not having children of their own, took aspiring young musicians under their wing. One in particular was William Yeates Hurlstone whose family misfortunes and own

---

[109] CRO/John Francis/SC/939.
[110] NLW/D.T.M.Jones/2975.
[111] Ibid.

health problems nearly cost him his musical career but this was avoided due to the generosity of the Beaumonts, who being old family friends, provided both financial and moral support. Alex was one of his greatest influences and many pieces, including Hurlstone's finest and last complete orchestral work, the *Fantasie Variations on a Swedish Air*, were dedicated to him. In his obituary from *The Musical Times*, Alex was described as a 'clever amateur musician – who will be remembered with gratitude by many young musicians for his generous and timely help ...' Captain Beaumont's services to music were recognised when he was presented with the Freedom of the City of London in September 1910. [112]

Amy Trevanion Graves-Sawle, youngest daughter of Juliana and Thomas Graves-Sawle, married William Prinn Noon on 20th June 1892 at Alphington, Exeter. Amy was given away by her father and wore a travelling dress of cream-coloured beaded crepon, trimmed with gold and lace, with a bonnet to match decorated with diamond jewellery. After the wedding ceremony, the happy couple left for Torquay for a few days before starting for the continent, en-route for Alexandria where William rejoined his regiment. William had received his first army commission on February 11th 1870, being promoted to lieutenant a year later and by 1897 had advanced to the rank of lieutenant-colonel. He saw active service in 1879 with the transport staff during the Afghan war and was present at the occupation of Candahar as well as at Ahmed Kheyl. There he received the Afghan medal with clasp. A daughter was born whilst in India in 1893, christened Amy Elizabeth but known as Elly within the family. During his later career, William was in command of the depot at Exeter. In 1906, William and his family moved to Plymouth to retire, purchasing a house called Hillsden, quite suddenly though, much to the shock and horror of his family, William died at the age of fifty-nine in 1909.

All of the family had been close, and following William's death, Amy and her young daughter grew closer to Julia Eleanor and her husband Francis Rashleigh Rodd. Much time was spent at their home, Trebartha Hall, enjoying the social life of early twentieth century Cornwall. Francis was the eldest son of Mr and Mrs Rodd of Trebartha Hall, Launceston. He was educated at Eton and Christ Church, Oxford before succeeding to the Trebartha Estate in 1880. Early in his life, Francis was made a magistrate for Cornwall, despite an early childhood accident which left him nearly blind. He was constantly reading and

---

[112] *The Musical Times,* Vol. 54, No. 848 (Oct. 1, 1913), pp. 662.

Fig. 69. *Elly Noon at a church garden party in Cornwall in 1950. She is standing second from the left. Towards the end of her life she began to give various items of family memorabilia away to friends and relations. Courtesy of the Noon Collection.*

expanding his knowledge of the world; a Latin scholar and an authority on history, geology, archaeology and ornithology, every species of bird was known to him. Fishing was one of his favourite pursuits and when his sight was good enough, shooting on the moors for snipe was a favoured pastime. Both Francis and Julia took an active and keen interest in their young niece, as they had no surviving children. Francis died in 1922 and was followed five years later by Julia, who at the time of her death had lived at Trebartha for nearly forty years. Her philanthropic work had endeared her greatly to the local inhabitants and her support of the Church at North Hill, Cornwall, saw her at her best. Julia had for many years taken a keen interest in the welfare of the building, donating a beautiful screen and stained glass window in memory of her late husband. Her five years of widowhood were

Fig. 70. *Pensylva, Kenwyn Close, Truro, home of Marianne Graves-Sawle and later her niece, Amy Elizabeth Noon. The contents of the house were put up for sale on 21st November 1979 and the collection of portraits, furniture and silver which had been passed down through the family for generations was dispersed. Pensylva was sold and it still continues today as a private home to this day. Courtesy of Jean Baker.*

taken with her sister Amy and niece Elly in Plymouth, where she passed away in 1927. The funeral took place at North Hill where the little church was packed with mourners who paid tribute to the memory of one who had been a great benefactor to the district and had won a place in the hearts of everybody during her residence at Trebartha. She left £14,241 in her will.

Amy Trevanion Noon continued at Hillsden after losing her husband, turning her attention to nursing and church work. Only a few months before her death she wrote to a relative of her hopes and zest for life, however, she was unable to walk far and was very ill. *'You ask if I go for <u>short walks!!</u> I am sorry to say that I am unable to walk like that, I wish I could, I am still an invalid, but was able on St Mathias Day to go in a car to* *church for the 12 o'c celebration, nurse one side of me and my stick! It was rather an exertion, but I was none the worse, and it was a joy for me to go, my <u>first outing</u>! I astonished a few persons who were there and the Vicar took the service, I hope I may be able to go again later on... I often wish my sister would have a companion but she sternly refused all suggestions! I have lovely flowers given me and yesterday a beautiful bunch of muscatel grapes from Major Rodd (Trebartha)... I am told it will be quite 2 years before I am well, I say "<u>patience</u>" everyday!!'* Amy died at her Plymouth nursing home on January 16th 1938. Her estate came to the gross value of £19,091, with net personally £18,896. A £100 bequest was made to the St Austell District Nursing Association.*

Out of the three daughters of Juliana and Thomas Graves-Sawle, only Marianne Rose was left. Throughout her life she had devoted herself to her family and subsequently never married. Following the death of her father in 1911, Marianne left Alphington for Truro where she purchased a large house called Pensylva. She soon involved herself with local projects and causes, joining almost immediately the committee for the Royal Cornwall Infirmary. St Kenwyn's church formed a primary focus for her philanthropy. She steadfastly refused a companion for years, although Elly was in touch with her elderly aunt regularly. She had visited the house many times as a child and she remembered 'in those days there were no street lights near the railway bridge in Kenwyn road, which meant you had to take a lantern or candle with you if you were going out after dark.' Marianne died on March 8th 1941 at the age of eighty-four, Elly inherited her whole estate, including Pensylva and the Llwynywormwood portraits.

By the time of Elly's death during August 1979 she was the sole surviving direct descendent of Sir Erasmus. All of the furniture not previously sold from Llwynywormwood was housed at Pensylva in Truro, the family portraits hung upon the walls of her drawing room. Elly was a strong and imposing character; in the local community she was fondly thought of but few dared to cross her. Elly was a great local benefactress giving profusely to local charities and especially the church. Just before the turn of the twentieth century, Elly was a young child living at Tremough House, Penryn, Cornwall. She would regularly attend a children's dancing class in Truro with her nurse. After the class was over and before the horse bus arrived to take them home again, they would while away the minutes in the building that was then nearing completion, Truro Cathedral. Elly recalled shortly before her death that she could 'still remember the knocks and bangs as the workmen carried on their jobs overhead, although I was not really aware what they were building.' The dancing classes has been organised for a few little girls by a woman who wanted company for her own children. They were held in the Women's Institute Building, in St Mary Street, Truro. Humorously, Elly cited that she remembered the horse bus so well because 'there was straw on the floor and it used to tickle my legs.'

Not long after inheriting Pensylva, Elly was forced to move out for the duration of World War Two as the house had been requisitioned for army use. It was at this time that she began a period of voluntary service with the Red Cross as a hospital welfare officer. She cared for sick service women and arranged accommodation for relatives of personnel on the danger list. At the same time, Elly began a stint on the board of the Royal Cornwall Infirmary which ended in 1947 with the advent of the National Health Service. Her keen interest in the hospital did not wane and up until her death she remained a staunch background supporter of the Friends' organisation. Flags were organised in aid of the disabled and also for Alexandra Rose Day by Elly who commented that 'people were very generous in those bygone fundraising days as, of course, they still are at the annual summer fete.'

Whilst listening to the BBC's 'Down Your Way' programme on the radio in 1962, Elly's attention was caught by references to the School of Infantry at Hythe. She remembered that a silver cup on her dining room table, which was full of flowers, had been presented to her father in 1875, whilst attending a course at the school. With no direct descendants, Elly decided to present the cup, which had been won for shooting, to the school in memory of her father. After returning from a holiday in France she formally presented the cup to the Commandant. She recollected that William Prinn Noon had been 'a keen soldier, spending much of his service abroad. He spent a time on the north west frontier of India, where he was in charge of the camels.' While being entertained in the officer's mess, Elly by chance saw a photograph of her father with other officers on the same course.

During the last few years of her life she became particularly attached to the vicar of St Kenwyns who would come to her home frequently to update her on the proceedings of the community. People who remember her recall a rather tall lady, of gravitas, living alone with a housekeeper who also doubled up as the lady's maid. Life must have been rather

Fig. 71. *The window in the choir of St Kenwyns Church, Truro, erected in memory of Amy Elizabeth Noon. Courtesy of St Kenwyns Church.*

lonely for Elly; her family had all gone before her and her position meant she had few close friends. She suffered from diabetes, which caused her much inconvenience. Elly bequeathed much of her Llwynywormwood inheritance to the National Trust. The oil portraits in particular went from Pensylva; portraits of Thomas and Juliana Graves-Sawle were sent to Cornwall and cannot be traced but those sent to Stackpole in Pembrokeshire included Sir George Griffies-Williams, Anna Margaretta Griffies-Williams, Henry Griffiths, Anne Griffies, Major Herbert and Mary Anne Evans of Highmead, and Rev. Sir Erasmus Griffies-Williams. A beautiful tapestry firescreen survives, which may have been the work of Lady Caroline Griffies-Williams herself. There is also a heraldic watercolour of the arms of the Griffies family and grospoint needlework of the Griffies arms, both are at the National Trust office in the King's Head, Llandeilo. Tantalizingly, during the residual sale of contents for Pensylva were two watercolours by Thomas Graves-Sawle, executed in 1870 of Llwynywormwood and of the park. Their whereabouts today are unknown.

The Fall & Rise of the Estate
1913 - 2006

Upon the purchase of Llwynywormwood by Thomas William Rogers, the estate was annexed onto the neighbouring lands of Blaencwm. On 7th August 1923 Rogers died and his wife Hetty inherited the estate. [113] By this time the house had been unoccupied for nearly ten years but was nonetheless still inhabitable. Hetty allowed the 1926 local sheep dog trials to be held in Llwynywormwood Park as no other location could be found. [114] On 22nd November 1928 Hetty, now a very wealthy young widow, married Morris Isaac but still chose not to reside at Llwynywormwood.

The Lewis family rented the estate for many years from the Rogers. Davey Thomas Lewis, was a founder member of the Farmer's Union of Wales, and had grown up on the farm at Llwynywormwood. During the Second World War the park was used for infantry, gunnery practice and training by the home guard who would carry out routines in the surrounding woodlands. [115] A barbed wire fence surrounded the mansion but local children were still able to go inside and marvel at the marble statue on the stairs, play in the cellars or carefully step across rotting floors for glimpses of the park from broken

Fig. 72. *The dramatic outline of the mansion house ruins as seen from across the park. Courtesy of RCAHMW.*

---

[113] H/MS/AT.
[114] James, Myddfai, p. 168.
[115] Ibid. p. 190.

Fig. 73. *The two end stacks of the mansion in 1979, showing how the central bay of the north façade had been completely dismantled, leaving a gaping hole in between. Courtesy of RCAHMW.*

windows. During the winter doors were removed for sledging down the banks in front of the house and it was at this time that the house was badly vandalised by pupils from Llandovery, who would come up at weekends and spoil the remains of the old mansion.

Hetty finally sold off the Llwynywormwood ruins to Davey Thomas Lewis and his wife on 31st March 1960. It was at this time that Penhill Lodge was separated from the rest of Llwynywormwood and was retained by Hetty. A year later she died and Penhill was sold to the Reverend Daniel Thomas. [116] Davey Thomas Lewis suddenly passed away soon after and the estate was put up for sale by public auction on 17th May 1963. [117] It was purchased by the Strouds who were farmers, paying £13,200 for the whole estate. The mansion was in a state of great disrepair, with its partially burnt interior left in tatters.

Gilbert Stroud fenced in the mansion house, filling in the Ha Ha, which ran all in front of the main façade. The old conservatory was taken down and the ice pit filled in, together

[116] H/MS/SAT.
[117] H/SC/1963.

Fig. 74. *A photograph from 1979 looking through the window at the front of the house over the park, showing the last vestiges of plasterwork in what would have been the dining room. Courtesy of RCAHMW.*

Fig. 75. *One of the fireplaces on the floor of the house amid debris of a fallen chimneystack, circa 1982. Courtesy of RCAHMW.*

with all of the cellars. On the wall of the staircase were the remains of a plasterwork relief that depicted the house in its former glory which survived up until the early 1970s. Most of the roof had collapsed in but the bell in the bell tower survived until it was stolen in the dead of night.

Whilst some first floor fireplaces survived, the ground floor ones had been removed many years before. Bell handles and other little house items all remained within the ruins. Even a Georgian flushing toilet was still in situ and in working order! Cows were kept in the bakehouse, which had been previously converted, but much of the mansion house

Fig. 76. *Another fireplace, hanging high amongst the ruins. It is interesting to note that this fireplace is still in place but in a perilous state of collapse. Courtesy of RCAHMW.*

was demolished and the stone used to build structures on the estate. Gilbert's father, Edward, removed the stones from the top of one of the chimneys to create a fireplace and grate at a farm in Llangadog. The Strouds had at one time over one hundred pedigree Charolais cattle and a flock of one hundred and sixty pure Suffolk ewes. When the former coachhouse was modernised during the 1960s, the floorboards were lifted up on the first floor and vast quantities of grain were found. It was during this time that the old bake-house was converted into a cattle-shed and a store for potatoes grown on the farm.

In 1998, Gilbert and Patricia Stroud sold Llwynywormwood to John and Patricia

Hegarty for £352,000; the Hegartys had successfully restored a house and garden called Hope End in Herefordshire and set up a Kitchen Garden Consultancy. Hope End had been given to Patricia by her father, and before her marriage she had attempted to restore it on her own. She was soon joined by John who also shared her dream that the house should be again lived in and the landscape restored to its former glory. The main twenty acre garden was discovered to have been designed in the late-nineteenth century by the famous landscape architect, John Claudius Loudon, who had installed varied walks with steps and stairways cut into cliffs and picturesque views over the three lakes. John and Patricia reinstated a belvedere on a cliff overlooking the house as well as erecting small temples and follies in the surrounding woods. A rediscovered plunge pool was converted

Fig. 77. *Taken from down near to the lake, we can see how the original designers quite cleverly placed the farm and outbuildings in a position such that they are invisible for much of the approach towards the mansion. Courtesy of RCAHMW.*

Fig. 78. *A view of the mansion house ruins from the carriage drive approach to the east. Courtesy of RCAHMW.*

into a romantic grotto, all adding to Loudon's original conception. John in particular put much hard work into reviving the one-acre walled garden back to life and full use. The Hegartys made a speciality of cultivating eighteenth century varieties of fruit, vegetables and herbs which were utilised in the kitchens of Hope End. In an effort to share the enchantment of Hope End with others, a small and intimate hotel was opened in the main house and became very successful, with one visitor commenting that 'there are few places in the British Isles which can rival Hope End's serene romance.'

Wanting fresh challenges and another house and park to restore, John and Patricia chose Llwynywormwood and moved into the old coach and coachman's house, which

Fig. 79. *The newly built main entrance gates into the walled garden, erected by Mr and Mrs Hegarty, the leaves had been blown into an unusual pattern onto the ironwork of the gates. Author's collection.*

Fig. 80. *The restored wall garden and corner conservatory built there by Mr and Mrs Hegarty. Courtesy of Mr and Mrs Hegarty.*

had become the farmhouse. They stripped the farmhouse of its sixties decor and made it into one of the most comfortable homes in Carmarthenshire. A period of thoughtful restoration and renovation followed which involved the removal of the mid-twentieth century render on the exterior of the former coachhouse and the reintroduction of the early nineteenth century landscape surrounding it. [118] Ten extra acres of land were purchased when they became available, bringing back in former parts of the estate. In 2001, Carmarthenshire Country Council granted planning consent to restore the lake, which had by this time silted up. One of the main focuses of John and Patricia Hegarty was the restoration of the walled garden. They partially restored the scalloped shaped walls and the interior was laid out on an experimental basis to determine the extent and variety of crops which could be grown again in this part of Wales using organic and modern scientific techniques.

John spent much time carefully analysing the remains of the fine landscaped park. He wrote that *'though the Park, like the house, suffered serious deterioration during the twentieth century, fortunately the underlying structure remains and since the Park relies more on its configuration rather than more ephemeral buildings, a landscape restoration project which is now in progress will enable many features and the feel of the eighteenth century environment to be revived.'* After nine happy years at Llwynywormwood, it was decided that it was time to retire gracefully to tackle a smaller retirement project: they had briefly considered restoring the old mansion and had outline plans drawn but it was decided this was beyond them, and left it for successive owners.

[118] *The Western Mail*, 23rd November 2006.

The Mansion House

Although very little survives of Llwynywormwood mansion, the archaeological remains are still rich and informative regarding how the house once was. It was on this basis that reconstructive drawings have now been made of the northern or main façade as well as a 'bird's eye' view of the buildings. Despite dating back to the sixteenth century in origin, only the bake-house survives. It is aligned north – south and was used as scullery, dairy, laundry and outer kitchen during the later half of the nineteenth century. Three bays are probably of seventeenth century date, but a further two are more than likely late eighteenth or early nineteenth century when it was extended into the bank of the adjacent hillside. Within the three-bay section is a seventeenth-century fireplace with bread ovens (see figure 82). However, all the roof trusses are pegged with lap joints at the apex with lap collars and tie beams of circa 1800.

Fig. 81. Looking towards the interior side of the surviving end stack of the drawing room end of the mansion. The archway on the right was photographed in 1979 retaining elements of ornamental plasterwork, see figure 74. Author's collection.

Fig. 82. Looking down from the higher ground behind the ruins of the mansion, the bakehouse range is to the left of the photograph. Author's collection.

Fig. 83. *The design process used to reconstruct the north façade of the mansion by the artist, Ceri Leeder. Author's collection.*

Fig. 84. *Ceri Leeder's impression of the main façade of the mansion as it would appeared circa 1812 utilising the archaeological and pictorial record, based upon the drawing held at the National Library of Wales (see figure 40). Author's collection.*

Fig. 85. *Standing in the centre of the ruins where presumably the principal entrance was situated. Directly ahead would have been the canted bay of the main façade, looking out over the valley and park. Author's collection.*

A three-storey, random rubble constructed gable end survives from this part of the house (see figure 90), together with a blocked-in seventeenth-century, possibly mullioned, window casement. This window faces north and is significantly higher than the later inserted windows. The whole structure sits on a levelled platform that is cut into a north-facing slope and has extensive views across the park. When the seventeenth century house was built its axis ran east to west, with a possible projection running to the north.

By 1729, the house was significant enough to be marked on a map of Carmarthenshire by Emmanuel Bowen. Although most of the houses are generic representations on the map, the choice selected for Llwynywormwood shows it to be one of middling size. The drawing shows a house with two gable ends, with possibly a projection coming out of the

Fig. 86. *The mansion ruins at sunset, looking through the trees from across the valley.*
Courtesy of the RCAHMW.

side to form either a 'T' or 'L' shape building. On a later sketch (see figure 87) there is what seems to be a mullion window that is partially below ground level. It is known that there were cellars on this side of the building so the window may have been an opening; alternatively, the level of the ground may have been raised to create a symmetrical Georgian front on the north façade.

It is possible that the Williams family extended the house during the early-eighteenth century, as on the eastern façade it seems that there was a window dating from this period on the first floor. The central wing also projects further than its eastern counterpart; was this section a later addition?

During the latter half of the eighteenth century, George Griffies-Williams radically altered the house. A two and a half storey north front was added to the western portion of the house, which included a round opening for what may have been a datestone or plaque. It was constructed using local coursed stone with well-cut long and short quoins to corners and chimneys, together with a limestone detailing along the base of the building. Surviving archaeological evidence shows that this was of two sections, clamped together with iron ties. Above this would then have been the render or stucco, which seems to have been quite coarse. In places there are the remains of slates stuck onto the exterior walls, which were then rendered over, probably in areas which may have had damp problems.

Only one contemporary illustration survives of Llwynywormwood mansion before dereliction (see figure 40). This pencil and ink drawing survives at the National Library of Wales and had been dated to 1888. Through research for this publication, this unfinished sketch was scrutinised and beneath the border of its frame was found an inscription – it

Fig. 87. *A close-up of figure 40 showing in detail the drawing of Llwynywormwood held by the National Library of Wales.*

Fig. 88. *Cilgwyn, home of the Gwynne-Holfords, was the principal mansion of the parish. In 1873 for example, Cilgwyn held 3820 acres around Myddfai. Author's collection.*

Fig. 89. *The semi-circular bay at Cilgwyn, the lead roof is similar to the one seen on the side of Llwynywormwood in figures 2 and 87. It is possible that the same craftsmen worked on both houses. Author's collection.*

Fig. 90. *Looking towards the gable end remains of the seventeenth-century wing of the mansion. Author's collection.*

Fig. 91. *A photograph showing the outline earthworks of the base of the south façade which was demolished during the 1960s. Author's collection.*

read *'Llwynywormwood seat of G G Williams Carmarthenshire'* followed by a date obscured by part of the foliage drawn around the house. A specialist in handwriting at the National Library confirmed that it did not say 1888 but rather 1812 or 1815. It would seem that 1812 was the most likely date as George Griffies-Williams received his baronetcy during May 1815 and the sketch distinctly states he was not titled.

On the original surveyor's drawings for the Ordnance Survey map of 1813 the house is shown but indistinctly, together with the farm and walled garden. However, the drives are marked and show them sweeping in front of the north front of the mansion. By the 1838

Fig. 92. *A modern day photograph showing the main facade of the mansion, with the home farm in the background. Author's collection.*

Fig. 93. *A close-up showing the fallen canted bay which formed the central section of the main façade. Author's collection.*

Fig. 94. *The remains of the late nineteenth-century kitchen range in the seventeenth-century wing of the mansion. Author's collection.*

and 1845 tithe maps, the north and eastern front canted bays, together with the semi-circular projection are clearly visible, together with the three-sided home farm (see figure 109). This further supports the accuracy of the sketch now at the National Library of Wales. As previously mentioned, Juliana, the youngest daughter of Sir Erasmus, recalled an old Welsh pedigree that was kept in the house; she went on to say that it was 'long enough to reach from one side of the dining-room, across the hall, and drawing-room.' [119] This in turn indicates the configuration of the main rooms in the house for any possible reconstruction.

The 1886 Ordnance Survey map shows there had been further extensions to the western portion of the house, creating a much smaller courtyard with the bake-house on one side, providing further service accommodation. The main rooms detailed in 1898 included the 'Hall, Library, Dining Room, Drawing Room, Servant's Hall, Butler's Pantry and seven bedrooms.' [120] On the 1906 Ordnance Survey map the semi-circular bay was then a conservatory, an alteration instated by Thomas Morgan during the late nineteenth century (see figure 100). The remains of the nineteenth century kitchen range also survive in part of the seventeenth century structure (see figure 94).

---

[119] Bayne & Pryme, <u>Thackeray Family</u>, p. 31.
[120] *The Welshman*, 12th August 1898.

The Estate Buildings

A planned model farmyard was built or reconstructed around 1800 to the southeast of the mansion. Today the buildings are relatively complete and in places some of the original cobbling survives. From the sale catalogue of 1909 the model farm consisted of stables, coach house, farm house, barn, beast house, calf shed and piggeries together with a newly erected corrugated iron stock shed. One range of ancillary buildings was contrived from the mansion-side to resemble cottages, to complete the yard.

The eastern side originally consisted of a three unit coachhouse or cartshed which was converted in the 1860s to the farmhouse (see figure 98). This was then extended into the

Fig. 95. *Today hidden in the woodland, Round Lodge served as the Gamekeeper's cottage as well as an eye-catcher for walks from the main house and park. During the demolition of the mansion during the 1960s and 70s, a significant amount of stone was dumped near to Round Lodge. Nearby North Lodge, although still standing, has been so radically altered that little of the external original fabric can be discerned. Author's collection.*

Fig. 96. *Penhill Lodge, the Gothick entrance lodge to Llwynywormwood, which was used principally as a private family and service access to the mansion. A tragic fire occurred here in 1845 where two young children perished whilst their elder sister was running an errand. Penhill remained with the core of the estate until 1960 when it was retained as a separate dwelling house. Author's collection.*

Fig. 97. *This photograph was taken in what was once the courtyard of the mansion house, showing the distinctive earthworks for early carriage drives and possible ornamental landscaping, 2007. Author's collection.*

stable and harness room in 2000 to form larger living quarters. Connecting the barn and former coach house was an archway, which also provided the main access to the courtyard; however, this has now disappeared.

Forming the southern range is the Great Barn, a hundred feet long. It appears to be the largest surviving barn of this period in the county, illustrating the serious nature of agriculture here at that time. It dates to around 1800 and is built of rubble stone with a hipped slate roof. It consists of a long single range with two entranceways in the northern

Fig. 98. *The farmhouse, which was originally a three-unit coachhouse but converted during the mid-nineteenth century. Since the demise of the mansion in the early twentieth century, the home farm has become the centre of the estate. Courtesy of the RCAHMW.*

Fig. 99. *Inside the long barn showing the triple purlin roof and pegged roof trusses. The barn is one of the largest to survive in the whole of Carmarthenshire. Courtesy of the RCAHMW.*

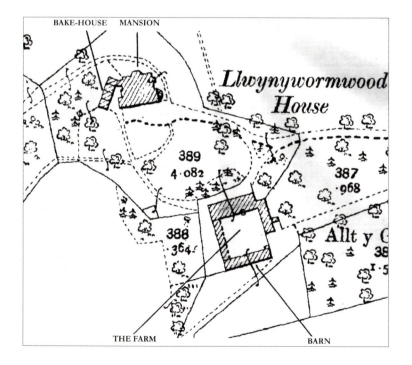

Fig. 100. *A plan of the mansion house from the 1906 Ordnance Survey Map, showing the layout of the mansion, home farm and complex number of drives and pathways. Author's collection.*

Fig. 101. *Three sale catalogues dated 1882, 1909 and 1963 of the Llwynywormwood estate. Author's collection.*

Fig. 102. *Looking towards the farm from the Lady's Walk, showing clearly where the fourth side of the quadrangle was demolished and replaced by modern farm buildings, 2007. Author's collection.*

and southern walls, the interior is undivided and the roof is made up of triple purlins and ten-pegged roof trusses of the tie beam and collar variety (see figure 99). Traces of former whitewash survive in part on the exterior.

Only the scar of the lean-to roof on the western side of the barn remains of the open-fronted cattle-shelter. It has been replaced with modern buildings during the late twentieth century. However, the northern range has survived in far better condition; the upper eastern section was a stable with loft over and was separate from the lofted lower stable end and heated coachhouse with dovecote. The space between these buildings may have provided an entry from the mansion house side into the courtyard. Originally there would have been five stalls and two loose boxes.

The Park & Garden

The earliest description of the Williams's park and garden was written by Richard Fenton in 1809. He refers to stands of old trees, which may indicate an initial scheme for the park pre-dating the late eighteenth century work of Sir George Griffies-Williams. The park today extends to around one hundred and ninety-two acres, occupying both sides of a small valley on an east to west alignment. The Nant Ydw rivulet flows along the floor of the valley before joining a tributary of the Afon Tywi. The parkland undulates with scenic drives, deliberate plantings, picturesque lodges, bridges and an artificial lake making it a delightful setting for the house, set up on a terrace above.

Sir George Griffies-Williams and his two wives created most of what we see today during the late eighteenth and early nineteenth centuries; their subtlety of planning has created an excellent example of a picturesque landscape. Richard Fenton, when he visited the estate, would have more than likely approached the house from the north. The Llwynywormwood entry in Cadw's Register of Parks and Gardens comments that even today, the three Brownian elements of grass, wood and water remain the dominant elements of the park which combine with the picturesque nature of much of the rest of the park. [121]

Sir George intended for the house to be approached from the north so that one would glimpse the mansion through the woodland by the twists and turns and risings of the drive as it crossed the valley. Thus, the whole setting became cohesive, displaying the

Fig. 103. *One of the early nineteenth-century single-arched bridges which transverse the valley floor over the Ydw. Despite forming an important feature of the park, the stream was never straightened or canalised. Author's collection.*

---

[121] Cadw, <u>Carmarthenshire, Ceredigion and Pembrokeshire: Register of Landscapes, Parks and Gardens</u> of Special Historic Interest in Wales: Part 1: Parks & Gardens, (Cardiff: 2002), p. 45.

house to the best advantage with the park and lake on approach. There are three approaches to the house from the north, south and east. Only two of the five lodges remain extant today; Round Lodge, which may have been built as an eye catcher and the eastern Penhill Lodge, which has been recently altered. The lodge to the south is no more than a pile of stones; likewise little remains of the other two.

The north drive or main drive is around three kilometres long, and when it was constructed, views of the house would have been obtainable at various vantage points. Some way along the main drive is the location of the Round Lodge, just as the drive curves

Fig. 104. *Estate catalogue plan of the core of the estate for sale in 1909 and subsequently sold off in 1913. Author's collection.*

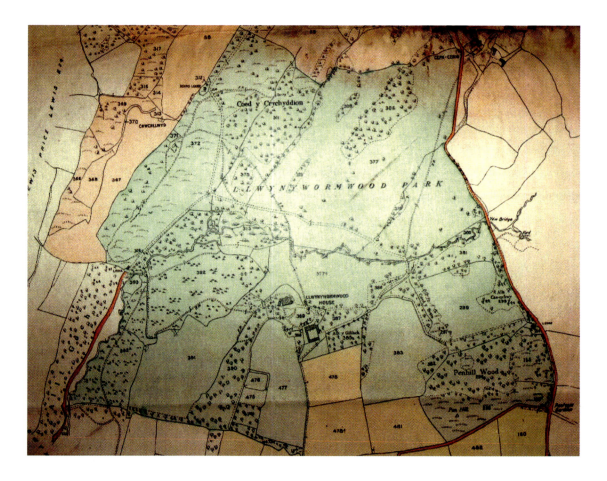

Fig. 105. *The main gates to Llwynywormwood which gave access to the principal drive that wound through the woods, past Round Lodge and then descended into the Ydw Valley, before rising again to reach the mansion and home farm. Author's collection.*

Fig 106. *These gates were removed from Llwynywormwood some years ago and have been reinstated at Lletty Ifan Ddu following conservation. Author's collection.*

around to descend the northern side of the Nant Ydw Valley by Coed y Crychyddion. Round Lodge is a delightful eight-sided building with a double pitched roof and may have been rendered and painted when it was first constructed. The structure was important for its position in the landscape as an eye catcher as well as serving as a lodge. Just beyond Round Lodge, the drive turns down the northern slope of the valley and from here, the mansion would have been viewed across the lake.

Many pathways were laid out providing scenic walks throughout the park. One of these paths from the main house down to the stream led to a 'Swiss' or rustic bridge to the east of the lake. Two other bridges survive, which carry the drives over the Nant Ydw; the first is a single arch bridge with a parapet, which carries the fork from the southern drive across the stream which is where south lodge was situated. Today the main gates are in private ownership having been removed to nearby Lletty Ifan ddu and restored. On the other side of the bridge is a carved stone with the date '1812'. Cadw believes that this drive was either a later addition or that the bridge replaced an earlier ford. [122] The other bridge is also single arched but is of a relatively simpler construction, although there is evidence

---

[122] Cadw, <u>Carmarthenshire Parks Register</u>, p.46.

from the rubble splays that it may have been rendered. It is suggested that there was a section of balustrading or an opening within the parapet to afford views of the park. The stream, it seems, was an important element of the landscape and Cadw suggests that it was never straightened or canalised. [123]   It is not known exactly when the lake was created, however evidence suggests it was during the last decade of the eighteenth century or at the turn of the nineteenth, as it was certainly extant prior to 1809. A survey of the lake has indicated that it existed at two different levels during the course of its life. At one end an earth dam retained it and the central section may have contained a sluice or small bridge. There was also an island on which an original planting of rhododendrons still grows and flowers.

To the west of the mansion was a small pond that had been created by the damming up of a steep gully. This was used for the collection of ice during the winter which was stored

Fig. 107. One of the silted-up lakes, with the mansion ruins in the background. The main lake dates to around the turn of the nineteenth century and was a major feature of the general landscaping. Investigation has shown that the lake existed at two different levels and in the centre was an island. Author's collection.

[123] Ibid.

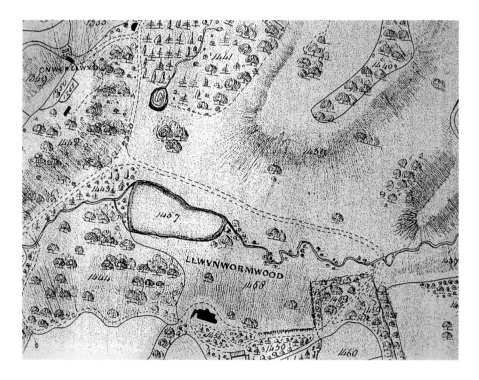

Fig. 108. *The tithe map from 1845 showing the extant lake with bridges. Courtesy of Mr and Mrs Hegarty.*

in the nearby icehouse. However, by 1906 this was recorded as being silted up. A rectangular depression cut into the bedrock is all that remains of the icehouse, which was virtually intact up until the 1960s when it was filled in. Gilbert Stroud remembers that even during a hot summer's day it would be significantly colder within the icehouse. To the south-west of the house is the small and interesting Walled Garden in the shape of a playing card, i.e. rectangular with rounded corners. It is believed to date to the turn of the nineteenth century and is contemporary with the extension of the main house by Sir George Griffies-Williams.

Mr and Mrs Hegarty believed that the tops of the walls were not flat but scallop-shaped. Originally, there would have been a 'slip-hedge' surrounding the walled garden to protect the south walls from animals grazing. There was also, to one side, an orchard and vegetable garden, protected by a windbreak, which is partially surviving today.

A Royal Home In Wales

Much to the joy of the people of Wales, it was officially announced on 22nd November 2006 that the Duchy of Cornwall had exchanged contracts with Mr and Mrs Hegarty so that The Prince of Wales would finally have a base here. It was anticipated that The Prince and The Duchess of Cornwall would use Llwynywormwood regularly whilst in the Principality and that the Duchy would build upon the great work already carried out by Mr and Mrs Hegarty. Following discussion with various bodies and Welsh language specialists it was decided that the amalgam of Welsh and English found in the name 'Llwynywormwood' should be altered subtly to the entirely Welsh 'Llwynywermod.' [124]

Further restoration of the farm and fine parkland were earmarked, with great emphasis being placed upon the employment of local craftsmen and use of Welsh materials. The Duchy decided that some conversion was necessary which included the rebuilding of the fourth side of the farm quadrangle which had been demolished some years earlier and replaced with a steel framed modern farm building. Conversion work began in earnest but

Fig. 109. *The interior of the dining room with lime-plastered walls and the magnificent timber-framed ceiling of the dining room were crafted together on site by local craftsmen. Courtesy of Wales News Pictures.*

Fig. 110. *The home farm and the mansion house in context from the east, showing the restored home farm and newly planted grounds. Author's collection.*

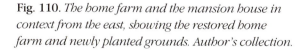

---

[124] As discussed in the introduction to this book, the Estate's name has always been fluid in its spelling and pronunciation.

Fig. 111. *A conceptual architectural drawing by Craig Hamilton showing a view from the north east, commissioned by the Duchy of Cornwall. Courtesy of Craig Hamilton Architects.*

was briefly halted when common pipistrelle and brown long-eared bats were discovered in an outbuilding. These were safely transferred to the nearby medieval bakehouse where the bats were able to thrive in a specially created attic space bat roost.

Planning permission was granted to enable a first-floor extension to the farmhouse, conversion of adjoining buildings to form a new dining room, reception room, kitchens and three bedrooms. The fourth side of the quadrangle would be rebuilt as a pair of two-

Fig. **112**. *The farm house, formerly the coach house, now serves as the focus of Llwynywermod since the dereliction of the main house. Courtesy of Wales News Pictures.*

Fig. **113**. *The original gateway and arch into the courtyard was demolished many years ago and has been recently rebuilt by the Duchy of Cornwall. Author's collection.*

bedroom cottages. It was also proposed that further modern agricultural sheds to the north-west of the courtyard would be taken down and replaced with a traditional thatched roof building. The Duchy of Cornwall stressed that Llwynywermod would be redeveloped in a sustainable way with features such as a wood chip boiler fitted to heat the farm, and Brecon lime plaster specialists, Tŷ Mawr Lime, would use sheep's wool for all of the cavity insulation. Local businesses such as Coe Stone Ltd, stonemasons from Neath, and

Camillieri, roofing contractors from the Vale of Glamorgan, also were employed. Welsh slates salvaged from elsewhere on site were reused on the new buildings together with recovered stone. Every interior door was made of Duchy of Cornwall sourced oak, together with locally sourced wrought-iron door fittings.

As author, I cannot forget that the inception of this book was due to the Welsh Historic Gardens Trust, and in light of this I have included a full account of the presentation of a special handmade and leather-bound edition of this work to TRH The Prince of Wales and The Duchess of Cornwall, which took place at Llwynywermod in February 2008. [125] The account was written by Michael Tree, Chairman of the Gardens Trust and was published

Fig. 114. *HRH The Prince of Wales being presented with a leather-bound copy of this work by Michael Tree, Chairman of the Welsh Historic Gardens Trust and the author, at Llwynywermod, February 2008. Courtesy of Mark Davies.*

---

[125] Further copies were deposited with the National Library of Wales, Royal Commission on Ancient and Historic Monuments in Wales, British Library and Carmarthenshire Record Office.

Fig. 115. *One of the more intimate rooms at Llwynywermod, which serves as a private dining room, showing the beautifully cut and laid stone flagged floor. Courtesy of Wales News Pictures.*

in their newsletter – The Bulletin. [126] The presentation coincided with a visit by The Prince of Wales to inspect the progress made on the renovations at Llwynywermod.

'Acquiring a new home, especially in a new area, is always hugely exciting. This is particularly so with historic properties where usually the initial decision is taken on the basis of visual appearance, amenity, and various other personal criteria. But only when the property is in one's own hands does the real excitement come about, when it is worthwhile researching the history of the property in order to understand it fully and hopefully to avoid making mistakes during the rescue process. All these came flooding to mind some little time ago when I heard that our patron, HRH The Prince of Wales, had acquired a new though ruined home near Llandovery. And so it came about that the

Fig. 116. *A view from the east with the home farm on the left and the mansion ruins to the right. Author's collection.*

Fig. 117. *Looking from the south approach at the rebuilt western portion of the home farm quadrangle, which had been done away with in the 1960s to be replaced with modern farm buildings. Author's collection.*

committee of the Welsh Historic Gardens Trust decided to commission a history of the property for presentation to his Royal Highness and The Duchess of Cornwall.

A very game Mark Baker, of Gwrych Castle fame, agreed to undertake the research and write the book at no cost to the Trust on the basis that he would retain the copyright. Many months were then spent researching the history of Llwynywormwood both locally, in Cornwall and in East Anglia. The results were far better than we dared hoped, in that we were able to commission a conceptual drawing of the house that existed on site up to the early 1960s but for which there were no known photographs. Also, a number of good portraits of the family were found in the ownership of the National Trust at the King's Head, Llandeilo, so bringing to life a family history that had disappeared from view for over one hundred years. The result of all this endeavour found Mark Baker and myself heading towards the village of Myddfai on a particularly bleak and wet day

Fig. 118. *Another conceptual drawing illustrating the eastern portion of the farm. Courtesy of Craig Hamilton Architects.*

in February of this year [2008], dressed in full winter clothing complete with 'wellies'.

On arrival we were met with the most efficient but cordial security which seemed to process us in record time. What a pleasure, therefore, it was to meet up again with Dr Manon Williams, our patron's assistant private secretary, who over the years has shown us much kindness and been so helpful, ensuring that word of our endeavours got through. After initial greetings we were then shown to the great barn of the estate where the presentation was due to take place. As usual there was the frisson of excitement and anticipation as His Royal Highness arrived. Needless to say, it was with great pleasure that I could on the Trust's behalf present the printed history which, by now, had been bound in the finest calf with appropriate gilding of the lettering. Naturally I took the opportunity to mention the keynote issues with which the Trust has been involved in the last eighteen months or so. And indeed I felt very proud to highlight amongst other issues the huge number of events the Trust lays on each year, most of which are of an educational nature. His Royal Highness congratulated Mark and I on the successes achieved so far with Gwrych Castle and Faenol respectively.

We then accompanied His Royal Highness on a tour of the building works currently being undertaken together with various officials from The Duchy of Cornwall, the Royal Household and Craig Hamilton the job architect, after which we proceeded to coffee and biscuits in a Portakabin, still in our wellies, and so ended a really delightful morning with the hope that the Trust's efforts really will be of assistance in the rebirth of a lovely Carmarthenshire estate by the very best of patrons a Trust could have.'

Craig Hamilton, the official architect for restoration of the farm, conducted The Prince of Wales around Llwynywermod and introduced him to the craftsmen and women working on the renovations. Both Their Royal Highnesses had been heavily involved in all aspects of the design process, from choosing the colours on the walls inside and out, as well as the finer details of the furniture and fittings. They were updated on a weekly basis with progress in the form of written reports and photographs. In particular, The Duchess of Cornwall chose the delightful overall colour scheme of duck egg blue, off-whites and terracotta. The interior has been furnished with Welsh textiles, antiques and furniture; a Welsh dresser presented to The Queen on Her Majesty's wedding day by the people of Meirionnydd has returned to Wales for the first time in over sixty years and took pride of place in the farmhouse. Welsh shirting flannel has been used to line the curtains, together with handmade Welsh blankets, quilts, and rugs purchased from Solva Woolen Mill in Pembrokeshire. One wall hanging should be noted as it is a fine early twentieth century Welsh quilt, which hangs superbly against its background of lime plastered walls. In the newly refurbished north range, there was placed an early eighteenth century Carmarthenshire dresser, decorated with early twentieth century Ewenny pottery. The magnificent timber framed ceiling of the dining room together with a large stone mullion Gothic window which looks out over the park were all crafted onsite by local craftsmen.

Fig. 119. *An eighteenth-century Welsh dresser which was presented to The Queen on Her Majesty's wedding day by the people of Meirionnydd. It has now returned to Wales for the first time in over sixty years. Courtesy of Wales News Pictures.*

Above the fireplace in this room is carved in Welsh slate, the three feathers crest of The Prince of Wales.

Work was completed during late June and The Royal couple spent their first night at Llwynywermod on 23rd June 2008 to finally be able to enjoy their new Welsh home after having opened the office of the Welsh Historic Gardens Trust at Aberglasney. Craig Hamilton has said that 'the project was intended as a celebration of Welsh vernacular architecture... it has been very successfully accomplished. The whole makes for a very,

Fig. 120. *The magnificent carved stone fireplace of the Dining Room with, above, in Welsh slate, the three feathers crest of The Prince of Wales. Courtesy of Wales News Pictures.*

very peaceful location.' During a speech given at Caerphilly Castle by the Welsh Assembly Government [127] in honour of the Prince's tenure as Prince of Wales, His Royal Highness remarked *'I tried some thirty-five years ago to find somewhere in Wales but in those days it wasn't so easy. At last I have a base. It is above all a tribute to Welsh craftsmanship which is of a very high order, and that unique rural and industrial craft inheritance that has formed so many equally unique Welsh characters that I have been so proud and privileged to have known during the last fifty years.'*

---

[127] Held on 26th June 2008. Speech extract courtesy of The Prince of Wales and Clarence House.

Appendices

A – From J. Burke, Dictionary of the peerage and baronetage of the British Empire, (London, 1845), p. 1048.

'Arms – quarterly; 1st and 4th ar. on a chev. engr. gu. between 3 bulls heads, cabossed, sa. a rose between two fleurs-de-lis, of the field for Williams; 2nd & 3rd, a2; a fesse, dancette, erm. between four griffins, segreant, or, for Griffies. Crest of Williams – a bull's head, erased at the neck, pean, armed, or in the mouth a spear, the staff broken, ppr. Crest of Griffies – a griffin, segreant, az, beaked and armed, or wings elevated, erm; the claws supporting a scaling ladder of the second.'

B – From Herbert M. Vaughan, The South Wales Squires – A Welsh picture of social life, (London: 1926), pp. 122 – 123.

'Yet another specimen of the squire dignitary was Sir Erasmus Griffies Williams, Baronet, of Llwynywormwood, near Llandovery. He was the last of the archaic Chancellors of St. Davids, and he usually resided in that ancient city. He was pompous, litigious, and by no means a general favourite. On one occasion at St Davids he stopped to lecture an old man for not saluting him on his daily walk:- "Do you know who I am?". "Naw", was the laconic reply – "I am Chancellor Sir Erasmus Williams!" (with great dignity). After a pause came the reply, "Sir Rascal Williams, and a fery goot name too!" And the old fellow proceeded on his way wholly unimpressed.

The whole family was notorious for its quarrelling and bad temper. When the old Chancellor died, his two daughters and co-heiresses, Mrs Beaumont and Mrs. Graves-Sawle, arrived at St Davids accompanied by two or three attorneys apiece; and not being on speaking terms with one another, with the help of their attendant lawyers they soon dissipated half their father's estate in legal proceedings. Old Sir Erasmus (nicknamed "Sir Crazimus," behind his back), though he was always putting pen to paper, wrote a vile hand. His letters to members of his own family were usually long and furious tirades:- "They are enough to blow up the post bag, my dear (said one of the Chancellor's sisters to a friend), but as none of us can decipher his writing, what does it all matter?" – I have a print of Sir Erasmus. It represents an irritable-looking old gentleman in full canonicals, twiddling a quizzing glass and with his right hand resting on an immense Bible.

Llwynywormwood and its contents have long been sold, but descendants of Sir Erasmus still continue in Cornwall, where his younger daughter, Mrs Graves-Sawle, resided.'

Bibliography

PRIMARY SOURCES

MANUSCRIPTS

AUTHOR'S COLLECTION

i. Letter from General Sir Watkin Lewis Griffies-Williams, 9th December 1870 to Debretts Peerage.
ii. William Gilpin, Observations on the River Wye, (London: 1782)

CARMARTHENSHIRE
RECORD OFFICE

i.   Census Returns for 1841, 1851, 1861, 1871, 1881, 1891 and 1901.
ii.   CRO/CAS/ix – pp. 1 – 13. – Myddfai Scrap Book.
iii. CRO/JohnFrancis/SC/761 – Estate Sale 1882.
iv.   CRO/JohnFrancis/SC/939 – Estate Sale 1909.
v.   CRO/Cwmgwili/Miss/II/186.
vi.   CRO/Cwmgwili/Miss/II/203.
vii. CRO/Cwmgwili/Miss/II/709.
viii. CRO/Cwmgwili/Miss/II/761.

MR AND MRS HEGARTY

i.   H/MS/AT – Abstract of Title 1959.
ii.   H/MS/L/51206 – Letter from W. Phillips.
iii. H/MS/SAT – Supplemental Abstract of Title 1963.
iv.   H/SC/1963 – Sale catalogue from 1963.

THE NATIONAL LIBRARY
OF WALES

i.   NLW/Cwmgwili/1515.
ii.   NLW MSS/4492D – Llwynywormwood manuscript book.
iii.   NLW/Cwmgwili/1526 – Amended Bill of Complaint from 1871.
iv.   NLW/CWR/SD/F/550.
v.   NLW/DolaucothiCorrespondence3/L3710.
vi.   NLW/Glansevin/2221.
vii.   NLW/MS/12357E – 'Bonedd y Cymry' by Alcwyn C.Evans Vol. 2 pp. 1385-1386 – Griffies-Williams family tree.
viii. NLW/MS/14897c.
ix.   NLW/MS/D.T.M.Jones/2975.
x.   NLW/MS/D.T.M.Jones/8076.
xi.   NLW/MS/D.T.M.Jones/8080.
xii.   NLW/MS/D.T.M.Jones/8145.
xiii. NLW/MS/D.T.M.Jones/8197.
xiv.   NLW/MS/D.T.M.Jones/8673.
xv.   NLW/MS/D.T.M.Jones/8703.
xvi.   NLW/SD/Ch/let/431.
xvii. NLW/SD/Ch/let/471-2.
xviii. NLW/SD/Ch/let/486.

PUBLIC RECORD OFFICE –
THE NATIONAL ARCHIVES

i.   PRO/Prob/11/1128, image reference 92 – The Last Will and Testament of Erasmus Williams.
ii.   PRO/Prob/11/1128, image reference 93 – The Last Will and Testament of David Williams.
iii. PRO/Prob/11/1854, image reference 293 – The Last Will and Testament of John George Herbert Griffies-Williams.

ILLUSTRATIONS
(Included or Referenced)

AUTHOR'S COLLECTION

i.   *MB/1 – Artist's impression of the double façade.*
ii.   *MB/2 – Tomb of Erasmus Williams.*
iii.   *MB/3 – Myddfai Church.*
iv.   *MB/4 – Gates to Walled Garden.*
v.   *MB/5 – Fireplace in medieval bakehouse.*
vi.   *MB/6 – Gable end of seventeenth century wing.*
vii.   *MB/7 – Drawing showing the design process of reconstructing the North façade.*
viii.   *MB/8 – Artist's impression of the North façade.*
ix.   *MB/9 – Rear view of ruins.*
x.   *MB/10 – Late nineteenth century kitchen range.*
xi.   *MB/11 – Ellie Noon at Trebartha Hall, Cornwall.*
xii.   *MB/12 – Drawing of Hafod, Aberystwyth.*
xiii.   *MB/13 – Photograph of Abercamlais.*
xiv.   *MB/14 – Engraving of Llandovery Castle.*
xv.   *MB/15 – Engraving of Lampeter College.*
xvi.   *MB/16 – Photograph of Sir Erasmus' grave.*
xvii.   *MB/17 – Photographic survey of the ruins in 2006.*
xviii. *MB/18 – Photographic survey of Cilgwyn in 2007.*
xix.   *MB/19 – Photographic survey of the Llwynywermod Estate in 2008.*

MR AND MRS HEGARTY

i.   *H/1 – The mansion from across the park.*
ii.   *H/2 – One of the bridges in the park.*
iii.   *H/3 – Mansion ruins from the east.*
iv.   *H/4 – Entrance of the Walled Garden.*
v.   *H/5 – Interior of the Walled Garden.*

CARDIFF UNIVERSITY ARCHIVES

i.   *CU/1 – Map of Carmarthenshire.*

CRAIG HAMILTON ARCHITECTS

i.   *CHA/1 – Panoramic drawing of Llwynywermod.*
ii.   *CHA/2 – View from the north east.*
iii.   *Eastern portion of the farm.*

THE NATIONAL LIBRARY OF WALES

i.   *NLW/D/8085 – Drawing of Llwynywormwood by an unknown artist dated 1812? – entitled 'Llwynywormwood seat of Sir G G Williams Carmarthenshire'.*

THE NATIONAL TRUST

N.B. – All received by the National Trust from Miss A.E. Noon of Pensylva, Kenwyn Close, Truro, Cornwall in August 1979.

i.   *KHL/P1 – Rev. Sir Erasmus Griffies-Williams, 2nd Baronet of Llwynywormwood, three quarter length oil portrait by E.U Eddis of 7 Harley Street. This picture was recently restored by Rachel Howells and now hangs in the entrance hall of the National Trust Office, The Kings Head, Llandeilo.*
ii.   *KHL/P2 – Anna Margaretta Griffies-Williams (Nee Evans), three quarter length oil portrait by an unknown artist.*
iii.   *KHL/P5 – Sir George Griffies-Williams? 1st Baronet of Llwynywormwood, a provincial full length oil portrait by an unknown artist.*
iv.   *KHL/T2 – Grospoint needlework tapestry, used as a fire screen depicting the arms of Llwynywormwood with the family motto 'Cryf ei Ffydd', possibly executed by Lady Caroline Griffies-Williams.*
v.   *KHL/P5 – Anne Griffies.*
vi.   *KHL/P5 – Henry Griffiths.*
vii.   *Watercolour of the Griffies-Williams coat of arms.*
viii.   *Portrait of Mary Anne Evans.*
ix.   *Needlework showing the Griffies-Williams coat of arms.*

The Noon Collection

i. NC/1 – *Miniature of a member of the Williams family.*
ii. NC/2 – *Miniature of Jane Lewes.*
iii. NC/3 – *Miniature of a member of the Griffies-Williams family.*
iv. NC/4 – *Miniature of Anne Griffies.*
v. NC/5 – *Anne Griffies drawing.*
vi. NC/6 – *Henry Griffiths drawing.*
vii. NC/7 – *Anne Griffies oil painting.*
viii. NC/8 – *Henry Griffiths oil painting.*
ix. NC/9 – *Miniature of a female member of the Griffies-Williams family with auburn hair in youth.*
x. NC/10 – *Miniature of a female member of the Griffies-Williams family with auburn hair in middle age.*
xi. NC/11 – *Miniature of a male member of the Griffies-Williams family.*
xii. NC/12 – *Miniature of Henry Griffiths Junior.*
xiii. NC/13 – *Locket with miniature of George Herbert Griffies-Williams.*
xiv. NC/14 – *Photograph of Lady Caroline Griffies-Williams.*
xv. NC/15 – *Photograph of Sir Erasmus Griffies-Williams' walking stick.*
xvi. NC/16 – *Miniature of Caroline Griffies-Williams.*
xvii. NC/17 – *Miniature of Juliana Griffies-Williams.*
xviii. NC/18 – *Tinted photograph of Juliana Graves-Sawle, nee Griffies-Williams.*
xix. NC/19 – *Tinted photograph of Thomas Graves-Sawle.*
xx. NC/20 – *Photograph of Thomas Graves-Sawle in 1903.*
xxi. NC/21 – *Photograph of Julia Eleanor Graves-Sawle as a child.*
xxii. NC/22 – *Photograph of Marianne Graves-Sawle as a child.*
xxiii. NC/23 – *Photograph of Amy Trevanion Graves-Sawle with her paternal grandmother.*
xxiv. NC/24 – *Photograph of Amy Trevanion Graves-Sawle as a young woman.*
xxv. NC/25 – *Engagement photograph of Amy Trevanion Graves-Sawle.*
xxvi. NC/26 – *Signed photographed of Julia Eleanor Graves-Sawle.*
xxvii. NC/27 – *Photograph of William Prinn Noon.*
xxviii. NC/28 – *Amy Trevanion Noon with her daughter, Amy Elizabeth Noon.*
xxix. NC/29 – *Amy Elizabeth Noon with her pet dogs.*
xxx. NC/30 – *Amy Elizabeth Noon in 1914.*
xxxi. NC/31 – *Julia Eleanor Rodd's graveside.*
xxxii. NC/32 – *Amy Elizabeth Noon in 1950.*
xxxiii. NC/33 – *Lady Caroline Griffies-William's lock of hair.*

Royal Commission on the Ancient and Historical Monuments of Wales

i. C10870 – *Photograph of the window of the Drawing Room, showing the last vestiges of plasterwork in 1979. Copied from the original loaned by Thomas Lloyd.*
ii. DS2005_043_003 – *Photograph of barn interior.*
iii. DS2005_044_002 – *Photograph of the former coachhouse.*
iv. *Outline of the mansion house ruins.*
v. *Gable ends of the mansion.*
vi. *Fireplace on the floor of the ruins.*
vii. *Fireplace in situ.*
viii. *View of the ruins from the park.*
ix. *Main facade in ruin.*
x. *Ruins at sunset.*
xi. *Fireplace at Llwynywormwood in 1979.*

Thomas Lloyd

i. TL/1 – *Bookplate of Sir George Griffies-Williams.*
ii. TL/2 – *Watercolour of Llwynywormwood, circa 1870.*

Wales News Pictures

i. WNP – *Photographic survey of Llwynywermod in 2008.*

OTHER

iii.   *JB/1 – Pensylva, Kenwyn Close, Truro –*
      Courtesy of Jean Baker.
iv.   *JB/2 – Memorial window to Amy Elizabeth Noon –*
      Courtesy of Jean Baker.
v.   *KC/1 – 'Last Supper' needlepoint –*
      Courtesy of St Kenwyns Church.
vi.   *KC/2 – Exterior of St Kenwyns Church –*
      Courtesy of St Kenwyns Church.
vii.   *SDC/1 – Engraving of Sir Erasmus' portrait –*
      Courtesy of St Davids Cathedral.
viii.   *MD/1 – Photograph of book presentation –*
      Courtesy of Mark Davies Photography.

MAPS AND PLANS

i.   *CA/1 – Tithe map from 1845.*
ii.   *CRO/SC/939 – Plan of the central portion of the*
      Llwynywormwood Estate from the 1909 sale catalogue.
iii.   *OS/1906 – 1906 Ordnance Survey map –*
      Courtesy of HMSO.

MAGAZINES AND NEWSPAPERS

i.   *Bath Chronicle.*
ii.   *Carmarthen Journal.*
iii.   *The Gentlemen's Magazine.*
iv.   *The Times.*
v.   *The Welshman.*
vi.   *The Western Mail.*

REPORTS

i.   *The Annual Register, or a View of the History and*
      Politics of the Year 1849, London: 1850.
ii.   *Cambria Archaeology – Tir Gofal Farm Visit Report*
      on Llwynywormwood January 2001.
iii.   *Royal Commission on Lands in Wales and*
      Monmouthshire. Minutes of evidence taken before
      the Royal Commission on Lands in Wales and
      Monmouthshire – Volume III, (1895, London).

PRIVATE PUBLICATIONS AND MEMOIRS

i.   *Alicia Bayne & Jane Townley Pryme, Memorials of*
      the Thackeray Family, (London, 1879).

SECONDARY SOURCES

JOURNAL ARTICLES

i.   *Carmarthen Antiquarian Society Transactions.*
ii.   *Roger L. Brown, 'A squabbling Squarson and a*
      contentious Chancellor', The journal of the
      Pembrokeshire historical society, VIII (1998 - 1999),
      pp. 27 – 48.
iii.   *Journal of the historical society of the Church*
      in Wales.

PUBLICATIONS

i.   *J. Burke, Dictionary of the Peerage and Baronetage*
      of the British Empire, (London: 1845).
ii.   *Cadw, Carmarthenshire, Ceredigion and*
      Pembrokeshire: Register of Landscapes, Parks and
      Gardens of Special Historic Interest in Wales: Part 1:
      Parks & Gardens, (Cardiff: 2002).
iii.   *Richard Fenton, (John Fisher Eds.), Tours in Wales –*
      1804 – 1813, (London: 1917).
iv.   *A. C. Fox-Davies, Armorial families: a directory of*
      some gentlemen of coat-armour, showing which
      arms in use at the moment are borne by legal
      authority, (Edinburgh: 1898).
v.   *Lesley Gordon, A country herbal, (London: 1980).*
vi.   *David B. James, Myddfai: Its land and peoples*
      (Aberystwyth, 1991).
vii.   *Francis Jones, Historic Carmarthenshire homes and*
      their families, (Carmarthen: 1987).
viii.   *Samuel Lewis, A Topographical Dictionary of Wales,*
      (London: 1845).
ix.   *Sir John E. Lloyd, A history of Carmarthenshire*
      Vol. II, (Cardiff: 1935).
x.   *E.N. Nares, Pleasant Memories of Eminent*
      Churchmen, (Carmarthen: 1890).
xi.   *Thomas Nicolas, Annals and Antiquities of the*
      Counties and County Families of Wales,
      (London: 1872).
xii.   *Kay N. Sanecki, History of the English herb garden,*
      (London: 1992).
xiii.   *Herbert M. Vaughan, The South Wales Squires –*
      A Welsh picture of social life, (London: 1926).